Great Welsh Number 10s

Welsh Fly-Halves 1947–1999

Great Welsh Number 10s

Welsh Fly-Halves 1947–1999

Lynn Davies

y Lolfa

The publishers wish to acknowledge the support of
Cyngor Llyfrau Cymru

Cover design: Y Lolfa
Cover photo: Getty Images

ISBN: 978 1 84771 708 5

FSC

Published and printed in Wales
on paper from well maintained forests by
Y Lolfa Cyf., Talybont, Ceredigion SY24 5HE
e-mail ylolfa@ylolfa.com
website www.ylolfa.com
tel 01970 832 304
fax 832 782

ACKNOWLEDGEMENTS

I WOULD LIKE to thank the following for their contributions to the publication of this book: the staff at the National Library of Wales for their willing pursuit of required research material; Clive Rowlands for writing the Foreword to this publication and for his valued opinions on the completed work; the staff at Y Lolfa for their cooperation and in particular Eirian Jones for her much appreciated editorial guidance.

Lynn Davies
September 2013

CONTENTS

FOREWORD

As a player, coach and manager with Wales and the British and Irish Lions, I worked with very many of the players featured in *Great Welsh Number 10s*. Recalling their exploits, as noted by Lynn Davies in this publication, gave me much pleasure and I'm sure that rugby followers generally will take great enjoyment from the following chapters. Similarly, in the case of younger generations, learning of the contributions of such esteemed international fly-halves to the game of rugby in Wales will be a source of immense inspiration.

Clive Rowlands

INTRODUCTION

E VER SINCE THE brothers David and Evan James, who played for Swansea and Wales, were credited with establishing the specialised position of outside-half towards the end of the 19th century, we have succeeded in producing a seemingly endless supply of talented players to play in that position, which, of course, is also referred to in the world of rugby as stand-off, fly-half, pivot, first five-eighth and number ten (previously known as number six). Indeed, mainly as result of a ballad written by Max Boyce, the idea that we had an underground factory that produced young men to play fly-half for Wales, became enshrined in our folk-lore. However that factory is no longer in operation and the demand for the product for which it became famous is now redundant. The old conveyor belt is no longer working. The patent is now defunct. The whole business has been taken over by multinationals. This publication endeavours to examine the factory's order book over the latter part of its existence, namely from 1947–99, until immediately after the advent of professionalism in rugby. It notes all the players who were capped at outside-half for Wales during that period, giving a synopsis of their careers and contribution to Welsh rugby.

As a nation we have attributed greater importance to the outside-half position than any other (contrary to the values lauded by rugby enthusiasts in other countries e.g. New Zealand and South Africa, where, during the time span recognised in this publication, aspects of forward play were traditionally a source of greater reverence). He was the playmaker and controller around whom the performance of the team usually revolved and the one who normally dictated the tactics to be deployed by the team. Of course there were occasions when he was the less dominant partner of a half-back pairing but generally it was he who instigated much of the enterprising play that inspired his team and entertained and excited spectators. Indeed, he was generally viewed as the great provider of a team's success in whom the expectations of supporters were firmly rooted. He was consequently eagerly exalted, giving rise perhaps to the claim made by Mike Gibson, the former celebrated Irish international and British Lion that "the traditional Welsh outside-half had the inherent ability to walk on water!"

He was the epitome of what in latter years became known as 'the Welsh way', in pursuit of which he would display innate skills which seemed to form part of his genetic make-up. Yet despite their common goal the talents of the outside-halves who represented their country over the years were varied and sometimes contrasting, as were the opinions of their supporters when advocating the qualities which merited their selection for Wales. No other position was ever the cause of such fierce debate among rugby followers and over the years arguments concerning, for example, Cleaver v Davies, Watkins v John, Bennett v Bevan, Davies v Dacey etc. dominated rugby discussion in pubs, clubs and the press. However, despite the regal status awarded fly-halves in rugby circles, they were often pilloried when they fell short of providing anticipated glory. This is born out by a frequently aired comment, when the national team was going through a particularly barren spell in the 1980s, that the remedy normally applied by the selectors following a bad performance by Wales was to change the outside-half!

Even though Welsh outside-halves of old had their own distinguishing *fortes* and weaknesses, they could in general be placed in one of two categories, namely the 'twinkler' or the 'glider' and their characteristics were succinctly analysed by the author, Alun Richards:

"There is the natural instinctive runner and the 'made' player whose effort appears greater, who in some ways is more exciting to watch since he is a duellist and brings a conscious act of deception to bear when beating a man. On the one hand there is grace, the nervous intuitive instincts of a sleek and darting forest animal: on the other there is a mental calculation and usually a greater point of identification and admiration. The sidestepper at his best gives off a kind of "Look, no hands!" attitude. One has a cool, insouciant grace, the other is wound up like a spring. One deceives, the other humiliates. This first group I call the High Church outside-halves, the second, the Chapel outside-halves... Of course, the categories are not as clear-cut as that, and no player in this position can be fully considered without an assessment of his defensive abilities. The qualities can sometimes overlap so that some fly-halves become non-denominational, but the distinction is there and always seems to have been present."

Since the International Rugby Board (IRB) decided to embrace professionalism in 1995 the game has undergone many changes. The amount of time that players now devote to preparation in the gym and on the practice field has led to considerably higher fitness levels and marked changes in their physical make-up. Their ability, during a game, to cover incessantly vast areas of the pitch has now led to a capacity to close down spaces which would have previously been more easily exploited. Similarly, players are now more equipped to maintain such standards for the duration of a match so that tiredness is now less likely to be the forerunner of capitulation. In addition, the general increase in the bulk and strength of current players, aided by input from dieticians and nutritionists, makes it more difficult to breach defences but conversely easier to stem physical pressure.

Perhaps the greatest difference, however, is the manner in which the modern game is played. Whereas some present-day matches, such as the Wales v England 2013 Six Nations Championship decider and the final Test between the British and Irish Lions and Australia three months later, produced memorable theatre and excitement, critics maintain that generally in the game today spontaneity is afforded little rein and is often at a premium. Teams generally use a specific number of planned moves pre-determined by coaches and the norm on the field features a pattern of phase play which usually involves a series of rather static and repetitive collisions where bulk and power are of paramount importance in pursuing a principle similar to that found in ten-pin bowling. Even when the ball is sometimes recycled across the field to a waiting line of players, who are in direct opposition to a corresponding number from the other team, there is every likelihood that such formations will contain a group of forwards, which can exacerbate the ponderous nature of such a process. Resorting to flair and adventure is frequently further discouraged by a preponderance of ping-pong-type kicking employed to gain a territorial foothold in order to propagate the tactics noted above, as opposed to engaging in more open and inherently risky play.

Of course the outside-half still has an important part to play within the confines of such a game plan, all be it in a role which would be alien to the players included in this publication. Whereas he is still the controller and decision maker with regard to the way in which a team utilises its possession, the modern outside-half, as he endeavours to implement the tactics devised by the coach by calling the appropriate options as he sees fit, no longer has the freedom, space or time to engage in the kind of instinctive play which formed an integral part of his predecessors' armoury. He is also expected to do his share of hard-graft tackling in a manner which was previously considered to be within the ambit of back-row forwards. It is still within his brief to unlock the opposition's line of defence but such an accomplishment is more likely to be achieved by effecting space for other players rather than by his own penetrative brilliance.

The fly-halves included below all played for Wales in an era when they were expected to entertain and exhilarate while endeavouring to guide and control their team's performance in pursuit of commendable results. The following chapters describe the extent to which they succeeded in doing so. There are various opinions expressed therein as to who among them was 'the greatest' but if rugby followers throughout Wales were ever balloted on that matter it is more than likely that, despite pressing claims from Cliff Morgan, Jonathan Davies etc. the winner would be Barry John. It is for that reason that he is featured on the cover of *Great Welsh Number 10s*.

CLIFF ASHTON

THE DESCRIPTION OF Cliff Ashton as 'pixie-like' and 'elfin' by the authors of *Fields of Praise* is doubtless derived, to some extent, from the twinkle-toed, mercurial manner in which he could dance over even the most inhospitable of surfaces, as was witnessed when he first played for Wales in January 1959 (in a game which is mainly remembered for the magnificent debut try scored by Dewi Bebb to defeat England on the sea of mud that was Cardiff Arms Park). Cliff's slight stature and seemingly fragile build certainly caused him to stand out on the field amongst other more muscular participants, as did his custom of wearing a white headband, thus making him one of the forerunners amongst backs who were later to adopt that practice. However amongst his most distinguishing factors were his lightening bursts of speed and cutting breaks.

He was a native of Cwmafan, and started his senior rugby career with his village club before joining Aberavon. However he'd been playing for the Wizards for many seasons before making his debut for Wales at the comparatively mature age of almost 27 years old. He was the first in a succession of outside-halves selected to replace Cliff Morgan, who had been an automatic selection for 28 games before he decided to retire from international rugby after the last game of the Five Nations Championship in 1958. Filling his boots after such a lengthy tenure caused the Welsh selectors some difficulty and in that respect six players were selected in the fly-half position during the following four seasons. This was the precursor of a similar problem which was to occur following the departure of Jonathan Davies to rugby league some 30 years later.

Yet Cliff Ashton had a fairly settled period in the Wales side following his first game, in that he was the preferred choice at fly-half for five of the next six matches, during which time he played with three different scrum-halves. Ironically for his fifth and sixth appearances in a Wales jersey he was partnered by Onllwyn Brace, who played for Llanelli at the time but who had previously played with Cliff at Aberavon, when their roles had been reversed. During that period Cliff was the team's scrum-half with Onllwyn playing outside-half. Indeed the latter left the Wizards for that very reason, wishing to join a club where he could establish himself as a scrum-half.

Following his sixth appearance for Wales, Cliff was overlooked by the selectors for the next nine matches, to be recalled in November 1962, after the departure of the incumbent Maesteg outside-half, Alan Rees, to rugby league. In a drab 3–3 draw with Ireland, a game which had been postponed the previous season owing to an outbreak of smallpox, Cliff partnered his Aberavon colleague, Tony O'Connor. He had a disappointing match, in which he kicked ineffectively, was indecisive in his attempts to bring his centres into play and was unable to stamp his authority on the match in any way.

It was to be the last appearance for both half-backs in a Wales jersey although at the time they were part of a very formidable team at the Talbot Athletic ground. In 1960–1 Aberavon won the Welsh club championship with Cliff being the linchpin of an attack which crossed for 155 tries. Between 1957 and 1962, the club supplied nine players for the Wales team yet Cliff was considered to be such a key member of the side that amongst local supporters the club was affectionately known as Aberashton! He was a popular figure also at social events for he and his club colleague and contemporary in the Wales team, winger John Collins, were apparently much in demand as a highly amusing double-act on the piano. However Cliff left the Wizards in 1962 and made one appearance for Newport against Bristol. The following year he joined Cardiff where he stayed for two seasons before moving to Chepstow Rugby Club where he remained for several years as a player and coach. A teacher and PT instructor by profession, he died in 2001 in Newport at the age of 68.

PHIL BENNETT

PHILLIP BENNETT WAS raised in Felinfoel, the village near Llanelli with which he has been inextricably linked throughout his life, bringing it greater fame than its renowned brewery, which produced Britain's first canned beer in 1935. He was not the first villager to gain national rugby status. For when, during his early years in the Wales team, he submitted a travelling expenses claim to Bill Clement, the Welsh Rugby Union (WRU) secretary at the time (who also played for Llanelli, Wales and the British Lions) for a 60-mile journey from Felinfoel to Cardiff, Phil was rebuked by the official and informed that he too once lived in that particular village and knew that the mileage to Cardiff was 55 miles, therefore the expenses claim needed to be amended!

On the occasion of his first cap for Wales in 1969 against France in Paris, Phil made history, for he was the first replacement ever to take the field in the red jersey of Wales as he took over from Gerald Davies on the wing. His first start for Wales was as a winger, in 1970, to be followed by a cap in the centre and then by his first cap as fly-half later that season. He then was a replacement full-back in 1972, which meant that he'd gained his first four caps for his country in four different positions.

'Benny' was a 'Chapel' outside-half par excellence. He was quick, usually running in a slightly hunched posture and with a concerned expression on his face, as he probed, darted and sidestepped his way through opposing defences

© Colorsport

with often pernicious effect. According to David Duckham, the renowned England and British Lion three-quarter, Phil was a 'typical' Welsh outside-half. "Invariably on the small side... he jinks, sidesteps with the speed and often numbing effect of a cobra's tongue." These remarkable talents were perhaps most evident in the scoring of three particular tries which, above all others, epitomised what made Phil Bennett one of the most exciting rugby players of the 20th century.

The first was for the Babarians, for whom Benny played on 20 occasions, against the All Blacks in 1973, when he was instrumental in setting up the dramatic score by Gareth Edwards which has since been invariably described as the greatest try ever. Phil, gathering a rolling ball in his own 25 while facing his own line, started the move with a series of breathtaking sidesteps, which took out a number of marauding All Blacks bent on hunting him down. This was the kind of situation upon which he often thrived during his career, whereby he would relish the opportunity to make something out of nothing. Following a timely transfer to J.P.R. the ball then passed through three pairs of skilful Barbarian hands before Derek Quinnell, responding to Gareth's shout of *"Twl e mâs!"* ("throw it out!"), delivered the ultimate pass which culminated in such a memorable touch-down.

During his career Phil was not blessed with an abundance of confidence and in the opinion of many his modesty was perhaps detrimental to his being able to capitalise on his immense talent. It was commonly believed, for example, that during his early career the undisputed flair that he regularly displayed at Stradey was too often lacking when he played for Wales. However at the outset of his international career he was, of course, faced with the difficult task of succeeding the legendary Barry John. In the words of Carwyn James, "Benny's only fault was that he lacked sufficient arrogance both as a player and as a person". To that end Carwyn, who had been called in to advise the Ba-Baas for that match in 1973, took him to one side and gave him the following instructions: "You're not in the shadows any more, Phil bach. Go and show the world what Stradey knows!... Don't waste any time, as soon as you like take them on!" He certainly did that!

By 1974 Phil's exceptional talents were lauded way beyond Wales as he relished the experience of playing on the firm grounds of South Africa with the invincible British Lions team. His brilliant 50-metre run to score in

Pretoria in the second Test saw a combination of fly-half skills at their best – a deceptive dummy, scorching pace and a scintillating sidestep. That score also led to his displaying a certain durability, a facet of his character which was not often evident. For in the process of sidestepping Ian McCallum, the studs on the boot of the Springbok's full-back ripped through Phil's instep, leaving a gaping hole the size of a ten pence piece which was gushing blood.

The reaction of the referee, on witnessing the damage, was "Oh my God!" while the response of his captain Willie John McBride was, "By Jeez, it's just a scratch... stick something on it... I need you to stay on!" Phil therefore played on with just a coating of Vaseline to ease his suffering (until the reserve hooker, Ken Kennedy, a qualified doctor nonetheless, was able to apply five stitches to his foot in the changing room after the game!). As if the foot injury had not been enough of a burden during the match, Phil was then knocked out following a blatant late tackle. However neither blow dampened his determination to continue, however painfully, with his place-kicking duties for the remainder of the game.

Despite his success in South Africa, Phil suffered the ignominy, the following season, of being dropped from the Wales team, to be replaced by John Bevan, but was recalled following a mid Championship injury to the Aberavon fly-half. Similarly, he was initially left out of the 1976 Championship squad, with Bevan and David Richards of Swansea being the preferred choices at outside-half. Once again, injuries to both these players meant that Benny was selected for the first game of the Championship against England and kept his place for the remainder of the season, as Wales won the Grand Slam.

His contribution was priceless and his 38 points meant that he became the first Welshman to score 100 points for his country. For the next two seasons, until his retirement from international rugby, he was elected captain of the Welsh team, during which period Wales won seven games and lost only one, and secured another Grand Slam and a Triple Crown.

Phil did not score a try for Wales until his 20th game for his country at Landsdowne Road in 1976. His next try, however, against Scotland at Murrayfield during the following season, was one of his most memorable scores and one of the finest Welsh tries ever. A move started by J.P.R. in his own 25 saw Steve Fenwick, Gerald Davies and David Burcher make telling contributions, before Phil wrong-footed the covering Scottish defence with a devastating and enthralling sidestep which allowed him to touch down under the posts. Almost exactly one year later he scored two more tries against France, after which he announced his retirement from international rugby. He had played 29 times for his country, scoring 166 points in all.

Phil also toured with the British Lions to New Zealand in 1978 and was given the ultimate honour of being selected as captain. Yet in complete contrast to the 1974 tour, it proved to be one of the most unhappy experiences of his rugby career. The heavy, rain-soaked conditions generally made it difficult for him to put into practice the individual skills for which he had become renowned and his confidence suffered. His performance and that of his team were often below par, despite the predominance of the Lions' pack, and losing the series by three Tests to one was a great disappointment, particularly after the success of the 1971 Lions against the All Blacks. In addition, off the field, there was often discontent, particularly between the press and the Lions management team of George Burrell and John Dawes.

There is no doubt that Phil became an inspirational leader of the Wales team during his final seasons and his alleged changing room talk, worthy of the most ardent of nationalist politicians, before taking the field against England at Twickenham has become part of rugby folk-lore.

"Look at what the English have done to Wales. They've taken our coal, our water, our steel. They buy our houses and they only live in them for a fortnight every twelve months. What have the bastards given us? Absolutely nothing. We've been exploited, raped, controlled and punished by the English and that's who you're playing against this afternoon! Come on Gar [Gareth Edwards] look what they're doing to your fishing, buying up rights all over the place for fat directors with big wallets. Those are *your* rivers, Gareth, yours and mine, not theirs!"

Following his last game in a Welsh jersey Phil continued to play for the Scarlets, which throughout his career had given him immense pleasure, for three more seasons. Having won schoolboy and youth caps for Wales, captained the invincible Felinfoel Youth team and played a handful of games for Aberavon, he first wore the Scarlet jersey during the 1966–7 season. He was also a talented cricketer and soccer player and had the opportunity to join more than one Football League club. However Stradey Park was his mecca and he went on to represent Llanelli in 412 games, scoring 2,532 points and crossing for 132 tries. For a record six seasons, between 1972 and 1978, he captained the Scarlets in their successful pursuit of a number of trophies.

The pinnacle of his career was perhaps his masterful display in the epic Scarlets victory against the All Blacks in 1972, ending with a particularly punishing right-footed kick from his own goal area, from a very narrow angle, to thwart a desperate last-gasp foray by the All Blacks in their attempt to deny the Scarlets their glorious win. At times fact and fiction have become intertwined when tales of that momentous occasion are recounted. Indeed, there are some romanticists who swear that early in that game, when Phil Bennett took the penalty that led to the Llanelli try, he *deliberately* got the ball to hit the post (rather than convert the kick) so that the All Blacks, in their panic, would succumb to the Roy Bergiers charge-down that led to that memorable touch-down!

Phil's kicking drew boundless praise throughout his career, albeit by virtue of his deceptively powerful right boot. It was often said that one of his few weaknesses was his ineffectiveness as a left-footed kicker. Similarly, his detractors would draw attention to the fact that from set pieces his distribution was sometimes lacking, in that he often tended to crowd his midfield partners, having too often considered the possibility of attempting a break. Such criticisms are soon forgotten when his accomplishments are recalled. In the words of Cliff Morgan: "He made the game so exciting that you'd have paid an extra £10 on the gate if you'd known he was going to be playing." The true value of his contribution to the game was perhaps best summarised by Carwyn James, when he referred to Phil's magical part in that breathtaking Barbarians try as: "A rare and memorable moment when a player is playing at a level other than the conscious, the unique moment when the game almost assumes an art form."

When he was just a teenager Benny was offered £4,000 to join Halifax Rugby League Club. On his return from the 1974 Lions tour, St Helens wanted to sign him for a fee of £35,000 over three years, as well as offering him a job. Regardless of these lucrative offers he couldn't bear the thought of moving away from his native Llanelli area, with the result that all such enticements were turned down. For most of his working life he was employed as a sports development officer with the local council, a job for which he was ideally suited. Since his retirement as a player he has been in demand as a respected journalist and analyst on radio and television and in 2011 he was elected president of the Scarlets. He was awarded the OBE in 1979.

JOHN BEVAN

JOHN BEVAN IS mainly remembered as a purposeful, direct runner who excelled at committing and drawing defenders with the aim of releasing players outside him. His precisely timed passing was also effective to that end, as was amply illustrated in December 1975 when Wales easily beat Australia by 28–3 with J.J. Williams crossing for three tries on the wing. Sadly, on that day, John won the last of his four caps for Wales, a total which would indeed have been greater were it not for the fact that he suffered badly from a recurring shoulder injury and that for a time he was in direct competition with Phil Bennett for the fly-half position.

In his early years he played in the centre but his committed running and tackling began to take their toll on his suspect shoulder. Even during his time with the Welsh Secondary Schools XV (for which he had been selected from the successful Neath Grammar School team), where he played alongside J.P.R. Williams and Allan Martin, he began to suffer from that particular injury. During his career he dislocated his right shoulder on three occasions, the first time when he was playing for St Luke's College, where he trained as a teacher, the second time when playing for Neath and then in 1972, having hit the ground hard following a tackle when playing for Aberavon (against Neath), whom he had joined the previous season. The shoulder came out of joint and the ligaments were stretched. By that time John had switched from centre to the outside-half position in the hope that such a move would lead to less physical commitment and consequently fewer shoulder injuries. However, the uncompromising way in which he played the game entailed that more drastic measures were required.

In June 1972 he underwent a career-saving operation at Neath General Hospital when his ligaments were surgically tightened. This allowed him to continue playing at the highest level for five years before being forced to retire as a result of recurring shoulder problems. After regular commendable performances for Aberavon, where he enjoyed excellent service from Clive Shell, he was selected for Wales B in 1974. This was followed by an impressive appearance later that year, as the only uncapped player, in the drawn game between the Barbarians and the touring All Blacks at Twickenham.

Despite an excellent Lions tour the previous year, Phil Bennett was omitted from the Wales team to play in the opening game of the Five Nations Championship on 17 January 1975, at Parc des Princes, with John Bevan being selected in his place. He was one of six new caps who contributed to a magnificent Wales victory by 25–10 and an enterprising style of play which resulted in five tries. The Welsh coach at the time was John Dawes who was an advocate of John Bevan's tactical *nous* and his astute vision in spotting in an instant any opportunities to move the ball to players in space (his perception at the time was no doubt aided by the fact that he wore contact lenses when he played, perhaps a comparatively rare occurrence in those days!). As a result, during the game in question, the Wales three-quarters, thriving on quick and direct possession from the half-backs, frequently breached the

French defence. In tandem with Gareth Edwards, he made a telling contribution to his country's attacking prowess on the day. He also excelled in defence whenever called upon and at one point, with the match delicately poised, he produced a fearless tackle in the corner to roll his opponent over and prevent him from touching down.

He continued to shine in the 20–4 victory over England at the Arms Park in the next game, when the Welsh three-quarters were again able to capitalise on excellent ball and score three tries. In the following match against Scotland, at Murrayfield, John once again dislocated his shoulder and was replaced by Phil Bennett. However he was back in contention during the autumn of that year to play against Australia but although he was selected to face England in January 1976 he was forced to withdraw through injury.

Bobby Windsor tells an amusing story involving John which illustrated the miserly officiousness of WRU officials during that era. As noted above all players could reclaim travelling expenses incurred when attending training sessions or matches by completing a form provided by Bill Clements the WRU Secretary.

The document also noted the mileage, calculated by him, which he deemed the players would have travelled from their various locations. John Bevan, on one occasion, apparently overstated the distance which had applied to him, with the result that his expenses claim was docked by sixpence (i.e. 2½p in today's money)!

He never played for Wales again after that game against the Wallabies but was selected by John Dawes, the coach, to travel with the British Lions to New Zealand in 1977. As was assumed from the outset 'Bev' served as understudy to Phil Bennett, the captain on the tour, and played in eleven provincial matches. He wasn't selected for any of the four Tests although critics were of the opinion that, in view of his personal form and Bennett's recent off-colour displays, he should have been picked for the final Test. Nevertheless he was widely admired for his purposeful and spirited performances throughout the tour.

Shortly afterwards, having appeared on 250 occasions for the Wizards, he decided, as a result of his susceptibility to shoulder injuries, to retire from playing and start coaching. By July 1982 he had been appointed as national coach and selector of the Wales team, a position he held until 1985, and expressed a desire to restore the glory of the 1970s and to have the team return to a more expansive game which would bring the wingers into play more often. However it was generally agreed that his aim of regaining Welsh superiority was hampered by a shortage of truly talented players and, under his direction, the team suffered mixed fortunes, with its overall performance being best described as moderate.

His style and methods of coaching met with sometimes conflicting reactions. For example, Terry Holmes considered him to be the best coach he'd known, although he was perhaps lacking in man-management skills (which didn't prevent him from being appointed assistant manager for the Wales tour to Spain in 1983). Eddie Butler considered him to be a coach who was ahead of his time and who wasn't perhaps given the credit he deserved but whose 'perceived truculence' sometimes alienated the media. However Gareth Davies, who played fly-half for Wales during John's tenure as coach, thought that under him the players completely lost their way "in a jungle of conformity, set moves and team work", with squad sessions turning out to be tedious and unproductive and Bev's dictatorial methods having a stifling influence on flair and individuality. In his desire to see the team running the ball from all positions John was, of course, in one sense undermining the responsibility traditionally afforded the fly-half for calling the tune and deciding how a move was to proceed. In that respect he remained unconvinced of Gareth's ability to conform to the coach's intention of getting the team to play a more expansive game. Their relationship suffered as a result.

John taught at Dyffryn Comprehensive School, Port Talbot, for many years. He was an excellent cricketer who regularly opened the batting for Neath and who was also selected to play for Wales. He was also a keen squash player. In 1985, despite suffering from ill health, he sought to extend his tenure as the Wales coach since he was of the opinion that there was still much to be accomplished. He was granted a further term of one year and endeavoured with quiet dignity to supervise squad sessions with his assistant Terry Cobner. However he was forced to resign for health reasons in November 1985 and died of cancer in June 1986 at the age of 38.

BLEDDYN BOWEN

B LEDDYN BOWEN HAD played 17 times for Wales in the centre before he won the first of his three caps as an outside-half in 1987. Yet his favoured club position was the latter having first appeared there for Swansea in 1980–1. He toured with Wales B to North America and Canada in 1980 and to Spain in 1983 before winning his first cap for Wales later that year at centre, a position which the national coach John Bevan had asked him to try. He had played nine games for the All Whites in 1981–2 before his work as a police officer led to his joining the South Wales Police club which at the time had regular fixtures with first-class clubs in Wales.

A former pupil of Cwmtawe Comprehensive School he represented Wales Schoollboys and Wales Youth before making his debut in senior rugby with Trebanos, the village in the Swansea Valley that has also produced Robert Jones, Arwel Thomas and Justin Tuperic. When he was first selected for Wales he was playing for the Police and all his 23 caps, except the last three, were awarded while he was a member of that team. His first game in the red jersey was the 24–6 thrashing by Romania in Bucharest, the heaviest defeat suffered by Wales in 14 years. For the first time the WRU awarded caps for a game against a non-IRB country and Bleddyn was one of six new recipients on that occasion.

He kept his place for the 1984 Five Nations fixtures when Wales, for the first time in 21 years, lost both their home Championship games. They compensated, however, with two victories at Murrayfield and Twickenham and during the latter Bleddyn had an opportunity to display his outstanding talents with a devastating dummy and break which culminated in a try by Adrian Hadley. The move underlined his *forte* as a superb linkman, a function which he accomplished with style and excellent timing. He performed these skills on the field with confidence and a certain coolness which apparently gave no indication of his customary pre-match nervousness. He also possessed a sharp eye for the break which made him a threat to any defence and, during his time as a Wales player, he crossed for five tries, two of which were from the fly-half position (which can perhaps be compared to the fact that Gareth Davies never scored a try for Wales in 21 games, while Phil Bennett did not touch down for a try in the Wales jersey until his 20th match). In addition Bleddyn's years of experience as a club outside-half ensured that his kicking was always of a high standard.

Peculiarly, perhaps, he was ignored by the Welsh selectors for the 1985 Five Nations competition, when they preferred a centre permutation which comprised two of Ring/Ackerman/Hopkins. He regained his place in the Wales team the following season and contributed to their success in the 1987 World Cup. For the next home match against the USA in November 1987, when he was selected in the outside-half position, Bleddyn was made captain for the first time and was the first police officer to skipper his country since Bill Tamplin in 1948. This was a duty Bleddyn also performed for the South Wales Police team that season. During that season he retained the Wales captaincy for the whole of the 1988

Five Nations Championship and his relaxed demeanour and accommodating approach, coupled with inspired determination when leadership was required, made him a popular choice.

This, along with the policy advocated by the national coach, Tony Gray and his assistant, Derek Quinnell, of allowing the players a freedom to express themselves on the field, contributed to the fact that during that particular period Wales played some of their most attractive and effective rugby for some years, particularly against England and Scotland. The performance and result at Twickenham had justified the coaches' attacking philosophy and their selection of four recognised outside-halves in the back line for that particular game. That season Wales won the Triple Crown for the first time since 1979 and secured a share of the Championship, having lost by a single point to France in Cardiff.

Bleddyn was selected to captain his country on the tour to New Zealand later that year but broke his wrist in the second game, which meant that he took no further part. The whole experience was a great disappointment to the touring party, in that they were obliged to undertake a senselessly arduous itinerary, succeeded in winning only one of their six provincial matches, were severely depleted because of injuries, lost both Test matches heavily and were generally outclassed. The knee-jerk reaction of the WRU was to sack both Tony Gray, who the previous month had been voted European Coach of the Year, and Derek Quinnell, and to relieve Bleddyn of the captaincy at the start of the next season.

In the opinion of Welsh players who went to New Zealand, and many rugby critics, this constituted one of the most reckless acts ever committed by the WRU, thus destroying the excellent rapport and highly promising groundwork that had been established in previous games between coaches, players and their captain. In addition, a consequence not indirectly related to such developments was the departure, in the coming months, of a number of leading Wales players to rugby league clubs. It was generally believed that such retrograde steps could easily have been avoided had the WRU not been so rash in deciding to tour New Zealand at a time when the Wales team was at a developmental stage and unprepared for such a demanding and rigorous challenge.

Bleddyn was chosen to play three more games for Wales during the following season, the last of which was against Ireland in Dublin, in February 1989. He played outside-half in two and was part, at that stage, of the attempt to find a successor to Jonathan Davies at outside-half following his departure to rugby league, a process which saw eight different fly-halves appearing in that position for Wales over a period of three years. Bleddyn resigned from the police force in 1988 and rejoined Swansea. However, with injuries increasingly taking their toll on his career, he retired from first-class rugby, after playing just two games for the All Whites during the 1989–90 season, to concentrate on his business career. Having spent over 25 years in the print business he is now a director of Infinity Document Solutions. He is an active participant in golf charity events and in 2010, along with other former Wales captains, climbed Kilimanjaro to raise money for lung cancer research at Velindre Hospital, Cardiff.

ROY BURNETT

His MOP OF wavy auburn hair perhaps made Roy Burnett, in the early 1950s, the most recognisable of rugby players but he also stood out because of his exciting and exhilarating style of play. As an outside-half for Newport he had been given the nickname of 'Twinkle Toes', which alluded to his dancing feet when running with the ball in hand. The wonder which that particular aspect of his play instilled in the Black and Amber supporters led to his sometimes being also referred to as 'Four Feet'. In addition, due to the panic which often occurred in opposing defences as a result of his dazzling bursts, he was known as 'The Ginger Terror'! Not that there was any aggression in his play, but he possessed a toughness which was not often evident. In one game against Cardiff, with the score at 3–3, he strangely opted, on more than one occasion, to unsuccessfully drop for goal, as opposed to creating mayhem with his characteristic electrifying breaks. It wasn't realised until after the game that he had been playing for most of the second half with a broken collarbone!

He was born in Cwmcarn and during his formative years he played for Abercarn Youth, the club which three of his brothers, and also their father before them, had represented. He was called up for wartime service with the Welsh Regiment at the age of 18 and broadened his rugby-playing experience while in India and Burma. Upon his return in 1947 he joined Newport (he had previously represented the club prior to joining the forces) and became one of their most loyal and consistent servants. When he retired, having played on the left wing during the latter part of his career, he had made 371 appearances for Newport, scoring 91 tries and 34 drop-goals. For the 1952–3 season he was elected captain, having fulfilled that particular duty in place of Ken Jones for most of the 1950–1 season while the winger toured with the British Lions. As a result of his prowess, Roy Burnett attracted the attention of rugby league clubs but all overtures in that respect, for example an offer by the Huddersfield club of £3,000 to sign for them, were spurned. He preferred to play for the fun of it while being employed as an engineering fitter in the steelworks.

His adventurous play made him a firm favourite with crowds whenever he appeared and, despite having British Lions stars Ken Jones and Malcolm Thomas outside him in the Newport side, it was Roy Burnett who was usually considered to be the main attraction. Indeed when a crowd of 48,500 saw Newport beat Cardiff by 8–3 at the Arms Park in 1948, it was considered that Burnett's dashing style in orchestrating a particularly potent Newport three-quarter line was the influential factor in ensuring such a large attendance. Although he could often pierce opposition defences with apparent ease, the notable achievements of such players as Ken Jones and Malcolm Thomas were due in no small part to the unselfish and effective manner in which he brought his three-quarters into play.

On 17 January 1953 Roy was at last selected to play for Wales, against England at the Arms Park, an occasion which he described as the highlight of his rugby career. He had been unfortunate in that, for some years, he had been unofficially competing with the magical Cardiff player, Cliff Morgan, for the outside-half berth in the Wales team. They had frequently opposed each other in club games and on many occasions perhaps Roy could claim to have had the upper hand. Yet Cliff, too, had all the attributes of an accomplished fly-half with the added advantage of being able to play, since his introduction to the Welsh team in 1951, alongside his scrum-half partner in the Cardiff team, Rex Willis.

However Willis missed the last two games of the 1952 International Championship because of injury. For the first, at Landsdowne Road, Cliff Morgan was selected to partner Billy Williams, Roy Burnett's club partner at Newport, who was winning his first cap. The team produced a great performance to secure the Triple Crown. For the next game against France at St Helen's, both Willis and Morgan were unavailable due to injury with the result that Alun Thomas, a former fly-half who was now playing centre with Cardiff, was drafted in to partner Billy Williams. Once again the team played well and a 9–5 victory meant that Wales had won the Grand Slam. For the opening game of the following season against England at Cardiff, Willis was still injured but Roy Burnett was chosen as outside-half as opposed to Morgan, a decision which few rugby followers in Wales could dispute, such was Roy's standing in the game.

The home team was unfortunately well beaten on the day with the Newport fly-half being given little opportunity to shine. For the next Wales game both Willis and Morgan regained their respective half-back positions in the national team and Roy Burnett returned to club rugby having won his first and only international cap. He also appeared for the Barbarians, Captain Crawshay's XV, captained Monmouthshire and played for his club against South Africa, New Zealand and Australia. He continued to distinguish himself for the Black and Ambers until his retirement in 1959. His decision to hang up his boots was apparently irrevocable for it is said that he threw them off Newport bridge when that particular time had arrived! In recognition of his distinguished service to Newport RFC, his numerous admirers presented him with a portrait in oils. He continued to serve the club as a committee member for a number of years and has been immortalised at Rodney Parade with the naming of the Roy Burnett Banqueting Suite in his memory. In 2012 the supporters instituted a Newport Rugby Club Hall of Fame. Out of a total of over 2,000 players who had represented the Club ten 'legends' were chosen to be enrolled. Needless to say Roy Burnett was one of them.

BILLY CLEAVER

William Benjamin Cleaver was born in Treorchy in 1921. He represented Wales on 14 occasions between 1947–50, although he had previously appeared for his country in six Victory Internationals immediately after the war. Following the resumption of official international matches in 1947, he played seven times as an outside-half for Wales, which was his position in a very talented Cardiff side, but also won almost as many caps in the centre. His versatility and his value to his country is further illustrated by the fact that he was also selected, on one occasion, in the full-back position. In 1947–8 he played in three different positions, for Cardiff, Wales and the Barbarians, against the touring Wallabies (who beat Scotland, England and Ireland during that visit) and was on the winning side each time. Yet he would admit that his favourite position was outside-half, for it was there that he could utilise to the full his particular ability to control a game.

The main reason for this dichotomy between playing him at fly-half or centre was the emergence at the same time of another exceptional player, Glyn Davies from the Pontypridd team, who vied for the outside-half position. Although Billy could be accommodated elsewhere in the team, he and Glyn Davies competed for the pivot position for many years and, as a result, were responsible for the first of many post-war debate concerning the merits of various fly-half pairings. It seems however that such disagreements were perhaps a little less civilised during the early days, for it is said that, when the chief rugby writer of the *Western Mail*, the renowned J.B.G. Thomas, opted for Billy when naming his choice as outside-half for the Wales team at that time, supporters of Glyn Davies invaded the newspaper's offices in order to seek retribution!

Having previously played for Treorchy Billy started playing for Cardiff during the war while studying Mining Engineering at University College Wales, Cardiff, where he had enrolled at the age of 17. He was also asked to captain the Black and Blues on some occasions, having already performed that duty with the Welsh Universities team. He was of stocky build, measuring 5' 9" in height and weighing 13 stone which made him a formidable tackler and a difficult man to bring down, particularly on the burst. In essence he was the complete footballer, possessing a very safe, quick pair of hands and a canny ability to time his passes to perfection, thus releasing his centres (usually the celebrated Bleddyn Williams and Jack Matthews in the Cardiff side) to enjoy a certain latitude which enabled them to utilise their talents to the full. He also possessed the ability to slice through opposition defences, using his bustling frame to the utmost effect to create opportunities for his centres or to score himself, which he did on 44 occasions in Cardiff colours. In addition he was a very astute tactician, adept at organising his back line with dependable control whilst always testing his opponents to the full with his own talents.

He was a superb two-footed kicker of the ball from the hand, being able to deploy this particular facet of his play to great effect, with ground-consuming touch-kicks, to nurse his pack going forward, to relieve pressure when they were under the hammer or to break the hearts of opposing eights as they were constantly forced to retreat. He was also a great exponent of the diagonal punt, shrewdly measured to put opponents in frequent difficulty. He was the first post-war master of the screw-kick which paid handsome dividends for him, Cardiff and Wales. All of this he accomplished during some six years at the highest level while apparently wearing the same pair of boots! Indeed, they were so effective that he became known as 'Billy Kick', although that nickname is thought to have been firstly attributed by jealous partisan rugby followers from west Wales after a dour muddy contest at Swansea when Billy was forced to kick repeatedly. This moniker however seemed to belie his doubtless ability to get the best out of his three-quarter line, which is illustrated by the fact that during the 1947–8 season Cardiff scored almost a century of tries, the vast majority of which were by members of the smooth-running three-quarter line.

Following the Welsh success in winning the Grand Slam in 1950, 14 of the team were selected to sail to New Zealand and Australia with the British Lions that year (with Lewis Jones being asked to join them later), for a tour which extended over 25 weeks. Billy, in recognition of his versatility, was seen at the outset as an utility back but, owing to an injury to the first choice full-back, George Norton, early during the tour, Billy played in that position in 14 games and in one as a centre. He was also selected for three of the four Tests against the All Blacks where he gave a very creditable account of himself in direct opposition to the legendary Bob Scott. On his return home he related how he and his team-mates had to quickly adapt to the unaccustomed rigours of New Zealand forward play. In his first game, having been tackled to the ground, a ruck immediately formed over him. Within seconds he was raked out on the other side and obliged to release the ball to the hands of the awaiting opposition scrum-half, thus being subjected to an early rude awakening with regard to the physical demands on players who toured there.

When Billy travelled to New Zealand he was 28 years of age and had been promoted, two years previously, to colliery manager in Newbridge, having served his apprenticeship over the years as a deputy, overman and then under-manager when he was just 22 years old. Like many players in the amateur era, he had to juggle the calls of his rugby career with the demands of his daily employment. During his early days in mining he would frequently have to work on the morning of a Saturday rugby match. Having got up at the crack of dawn he would report for the six o'clock shift at the local coal mine, walking some one-and-a-half miles underground to spend the next few hours undertaking his duties at the coalface and in general workings. It was then a case of rushing home to bathe in a tin bath in front of the fire before catching two buses to get to the Arms Park in time for the kick-off. When he became established in the Wales team he was excused from working on the Friday prior to an international, but was nonetheless expected to turn up for the early morning shift on the Sunday!

As a colliery manager there were other pressures on him. He was subject to regulations which stipulated that no colliery could be without the presence of a manager for more than three months at a time and, after the Lions had played the third Test in New Zealand, Billy was informed by the National Coal Board that he had broken its rules and would therefore be replaced by another manager at the Newbridge collieries. He had also, at that time, been chosen as captain of Cardiff Rugby Club for the following season, a position which, due to demands both on and off the field, would have taken much of his time. Since he was married with a young family he was therefore forced to come to terms with the fact that if he was to continue with his chosen career with the Coal Board he would have to retire from playing rugby, which he did on his return from New Zealand in 1950. In due course he became a member of the Cardiff Club Committee and was soon asked to take charge of the Welsh Youth Rugby Union. His career in the mining industry also blossomed and eventually he became deputy director of the South Wales Coalfield and retired in 1983.

He played just one more representative game, when he turned out for a British Lions side against Cardiff to celebrate the club's 75th anniversary in 1951. On that occasion he played scrum-half, for the first time in his career, with Ireland's Jackie Kyle outside him and contributed to a 14–12 victory. His success as a player and likeable personality made him a very popular figure at the Arms Park and his reputation was apparently further enhanced in the club bar on Saturday nights when, following home games, his angelic appearance and blond curls seemed to complement a lovely tenor voice to captivate visitors there, particularly when he sang his party piece, 'Macushla'. In later life he became a member of the Arts Council of Great Britain, secretary of the Contemporary Arts Society for Wales, vice chairman of the Welsh Arts Council, and chairman of the Butetown Railway Historical Society. He passed away in 2003.

TONY CLEMENT

H E WAS ONE of the most gifted of all the players selected at outside-half for Wales, for whom he appeared on 37 occasions (eight of which were as a replacement) over a period of eight years. The fact that during his international career he played in four different positions is perhaps an indication of the varied talents he possessed. According to some critics his versatility perhaps served as an obstacle to his becoming a regular fixture in the Wales team at any point in his career. Indeed his longest run of games was in 1991–2 when he wore the red jersey in six consecutive matches as full-back, where he played most frequently for his country.

It was in that position that he was first selected for Wales (he had won his first cap as a replacement centre against the USA in 1987) against England at Twickenham in February 1988, in somewhat controversial circumstances. For he was included in the team at the expense of Paul Thorburn, who had previously kicked 140 points in 15 games. Yet despite his prowess as a kicker and his defensive dependability Thorburn, unlike the man who replaced him for that game, was not known for his attacking flair and the Wales coach, Tony Gray, was looking to field a team which could play expansive 15-man rugby. With that in mind he included four recognised fly-halves in his line-up at Twickenham, namely Jonathan Davies at number ten, Mark Ring and Bleddyn Bowen in the centre and Tony Clement at full-back.

Critics pointed out that Tony's inexperience in that position (he had only played there once before at senior level, since he regularly played at outside-half with Swansea) would make him vulnerable under pressure kicks from England, and indeed that was a tactic frequently deployed on the day by Cusworth, their fly-half. However Tony dealt admirably with the aerial bombardment and, on one telling occasion, having gathered the ball safely and sped past a few would-be English tacklers, he launched a spectacular move, over 80 yards, which culminated in a try by Adrian Hadley and helped Wales to victory by 11–3. Because of injury Tony missed the rest of the season and Thorburn was recalled, but both remained in competition for the full-back spot over the next few years with the selectors often opting for the 'safety first' approach of going with the Neath player. Yet even after Thorburn's retirement from rugby in 1991 the emergence of Mike Rayer saw Tony once again having to compete for the full-back position in the Wales team.

However his value as an attacking player was accommodated at times by his selection in alternative positions in the three-quarter line. In 1989–90 he was chosen to play three times at outside-half, firstly against New Zealand and was voted Man of the Match by some critics, followed by two more appearances at fly-half against Namibia. In 1994, he was selected at full-back, on the wing and in the centre, the position in which he won his first cap as a replacement. Indeed on that auspicious occasion he scored two tries, which was the first time that a new player had accomplished such a feat since 1931. He, of course, also possessed the essential qualities of a top-class full-back in that he was a reliable tackler, had the ability to gain ground with hefty clearing kicks and had a good sense of positioning. By many, however, apart from his adaptability, he is remembered mainly for his exciting and imaginative running and his ability to beat opponents with both pace and guile.

Supporters at Swansea Rugby Club bore regular witness to these talents between 1985–99. A former pupil of Morriston Comprehensive School, Tony represented Wales Schools at rugby and Swansea Schools at soccer. He joined the All Whites as a teenager and played for Wales Youth, and later Wales Under 20 and Under 21 teams. He was also selected for Wales B and the Barbarians. Apart from a year spent, at Swansea's request, honing his skills with Poneke in New Zealand, he remained at St Helen's throughout his career, making 247 appearances, mainly at outside-half, and scoring 61 tries and 319 points. Having played just a few games for Wales, his attributes were widely recognised in 1989 when he was called up as a late replacement on the Lions tour to Australia for the injured winger, Chris Oti. He made only two appearances for Donal's Donuts, the name given to the unbeaten midweek team that played under the captaincy of the Irishman, Donald Lenihan, but cemented his reputation as a player who could play to the highest standard in more than one position. Later that year he joined nine other Wales international players on a highly controversial visit to South Africa to take part in rugby matches arranged to celebrate the centenary of the South Africa Rugby Board, for which players were allegedly paid sums in the region of £35,000, in breach of amateur regulations at the time.

In 1993 he was selected as a utility back for the British Lions tour to New Zealand, playing in seven provincial matches and scoring 13 points. He did nor appear in any of the Tests but was viewed as a replacement for the captain and first-choice full-back, Gavin Hastings, who had been suffering from hamstring problems. Tony also went to New Zealand with the Wales team in 1988 and played full-back in the first Test, which the visitors lost by 52–3. He was also part of the Wales squads in the World Cup competitions of 1991 (during which he suffered broken ribs in the game against Samoa) and 1995 and made his last appearance for his country during that latter event against Ireland at Ellis Park, Johannesburg, having also played in both previous Pool matches.

Following a period as coach at Swansea he became manager of the Wales Under 20 team, a position which has now been assumed by Mark Taylor. Tony is currently employed as a banking manager at the Swansea branch of the Swedish bank, Handelsbanken, having previously held finance positions with Inter City Finance and C.E.M. Day.

MALCOLM DACEY

N OT BEING A jinking, darting exponent of outside-half skills, the Swansea outside-half, Malcolm Dacey, had a classy, elegant way of playing the game. During his international career, which saw him being capped 15 times for his country, he and Gareth Davies were the subject of constant debate as to whom of the two was the more deserving of the Wales number ten jersey. Although they were not dissimilar in style, Malcolm was considered to be the better orchestrator of his three-quarter line to play the more expansive game favoured by the Wales coach at the time, John Bevan. The coach had always been an advocate of back play that produced speedy, direct running combined with good, well-timed passing which released three-quarters to penetrate and to entertain. In that respect Malcolm Dacey fitted the bill as the ideal playmaker who was also a solid defender. In due course Gareth Davies's awareness of the coach's preference for the Swansea player led indirectly to his retirement from international rugby in 1985.

Malcolm was the product of Cefn Hengoed Comprehensive and Bonymaen Rugby Club, from where he was selected to play for Swansea Schoolboys and, later, for the Wales Youth team, at both centre and outside-half. Having graduated to his local club's senior team, he appeared in October 1978 for Swansea against Penarth. The Whites at that time didn't appear to be keen to hold on to him, so he joined Neath Rugby Club. However the

1979–80 season saw him back at Swansea. He soon made an impression on a wider stage as he played for his club in the 1980 Schweppes Cup final and later that year against the All Blacks in the centre position.

He remained at St Helen's until 1986–7. Since, at that particular time, the club wished to play Tony Clement at fly-half, Malcolm moved to the Arms Park and played for Cardiff for two seasons. He then returned to his local Bonymaen club for a short spell, before completing his first-class career with a further two years with Swansea. In all he made 263 appearances for the club, scoring 269 points, which included 47 tries. He finished his rugby-playing career back with his local club, helping them to promotion in the Heineken League, where he also served as coach for a number of years.

His form for Swansea in the early 1980s soon attracted the attention of the Wales selectors and he was chosen to represent the Wales B side against France and Australia before being selected for Wales in an uncapped match against the New Zealand Maoris at the Arms Park in November 1982, when he contributed to a home victory with a drop-goal. Having had a decent game in the final Welsh trial he was selected, at the expense of Gareth Davies, the previous incumbent, as one of four new caps to face England at Cardiff in February 1983, in a match that resulted in a 13–13 draw.

He was renowned as a very effective runner who could bring the best out of his backs, rather than as a kicker, yet for most of that game he kicked the ball downfield in response to alleged orders to 'keep the ball in front of his forwards'. He held on to his place for the Scotland game (and for the subsequent nine matches) with the instruction that he should go out and express himself, which he did when his vision put Clive Rees away on a run which led to Elgan Rees touching down for an excellent try. Critics agree that his best performance for his country was on his first visit to Twickenham in 1984. By then he had matured into a shrewd and influential general of the Wales three-quarters and had been described before that game by Peter Wheeler, the England captain, as the most improved player in the home countries who was the hub of the dangerous Wales backs. He was so right! Benefiting from superb service from Terry Holmes on the day, Malcolm, according to one press report, 'dominated the Twickenham stage... with a performance that bristled with authority and conviction' and, with two drop-goals, ensured a Wales victory by 24–15, their highest total ever at Twickenham at that time.

When he withdrew from the Wales team with injury in late February 1985 he was replaced by Gareth Davies who retained the number ten shirt for the next three matches until he then lost his place to the promising Jonathan Davies, who made the position his own for the next few years. Malcolm did not represent Wales again until he played full-back on three occasions, against Fiji, Tonga and Western Samoa, during their tour of the South Seas in 1986. He won his final cap for his country during the 1987 World Cup in New Zealand when he was selected as outside-half in the Wales victory against Tonga and regained his place in the national squad in 1990–1. He won many other honours in the game, for example he came on as a replacement for the British and Irish Lions against the Rest of the World XV in 1986, represented a Five Nations XV against the Overseas Unions and played for the Barbarians.

ADRIAN DAVIES

A N OUTSIDE-HALF IN the classical mould, Adrian Davies was a natural footballer who could possibly have made the grade as a soccer player, having been capped for the Wales Schools Under 15 soccer team as well as gaining a Blue at soccer, in addition to his four rugby Blues, at Cambridge University. Born in Bridgend, he first made a name for himself as a rugby player while a pupil at Pencoed Comprehensive School and represented the Welsh Secondary Schools team. Numerous national honours followed, with Wales Under 19, Welsh Universities, Welsh Students and the Wales A and B teams, before he won his first senior cap as a replacement centre against the Barbarians in Cardiff in October 1990, at the age of 21 years. Such encounters did not usually merit the granting of caps but, on that particular occasion, the Barbarians were celebrating their centenary, therefore it was decided to mark the event by regarding the game as a full international match.

Having first appeared for Neath in 1987–8 as a teenager, he was a member of the Gnoll club when he won that first cap and, although the team enjoyed great success, it was primarily renowned for its powerful forward play. Consequently Adrian and his co-centre, Scott Gibbs, left the Welsh All Blacks in 1991 to play for less forward-orientated teams, namely Cardiff and Swansea respectively. Adrian enjoyed five successful seasons with the Arms Park club during which time he appeared in 105 games, scoring

1,162 points, which comprised 37 tries, 167 penalties, 18 drop-goals and 212 conversions. He won his remaining eight caps for Wales whilst playing for Cardiff.

His international career however was rather chequered in that over a period of a little under six years his appearances in the Wales jersey were rather spasmodic. He never played in the Five Nations Championship and, in addition to his cap against the Barbarians, he represented his country against Australia, Zimbabwe (2), Japan (2), Canada, Fiji and Ireland. Apart from his appearance against the Wallabies, which was in the centre, he played at outside-half in those matches. Following the encounter with Fiji in 1993 he wasn't selected for the next nine Wales matches, only to be recalled for two Pool matches in the 1995 World Cup, by Alex Evans, his coach at Cardiff, who had taken over in a caretaker capacity from Alan Davies as the Wales coach for the tournament.

Adrian didn't wear the Welsh jersey again and in 1996 he left Cardiff Rugby Club to join Richmond in the English Premiership, where he played until he was forced to retire because of injury in September 1999. He represented the club 19 times, scoring 175 points. After a brief period as coach at Esher Rugby Club he was appointed in 2000, at the age of 30, as Director of Rugby with London Welsh, who were in Division Two of the English National League. He spent six years at Old Deer Park and at the time of his appointment he was one of the youngest holders of such a position in top-flight rugby. He is a qualified chartered surveyor and is currently a director of a business development agency.

It was generally considered that he had been unfortunate not to have been given a run of games for Wales, which made it all the more difficult for him to assert his influence on the team from the outside-half position. In addition the performance of the Wales team over that period was rather erratic, with a 63–6 drubbing by Australia and a home defeat by Canada (during which he went 20 minutes without receiving a pass) being the low points of his tenure. With Wales he had few opportunities to display his particular talents, namely a deceptive, shimmying style of running, being always at the ready to strike suddenly from midfield with telling breaks when least expected and an ability to kick well with either foot. He was not however at his best when subjected to pressure, a weakness which was perhaps exacerbated by a somewhat laid-back demeanour.

GARETH DAVIES

G ARETH DAVIES, LIKE another Wales outside-half, David Watkins, almost 20 years previously, turned his back on international rugby in April 1985 because of the fickleness of the selectors of the national team. Whereas Watkins went North to excel in the 13-a-side game, Davies decided to hang up his boots at the end of that particular season. By that time, although he had always enjoyed playing for his club, Cardiff, he had become completely disenchanted with the game at the highest level. He would later claim that the main reason for this was that the Wales squad sessions under coach John Bevan had become a "jungle of conformity", with stereotyped set moves becoming the norm at the expense of flair and creativity.

Such a philosophy was completely alien to the way that Gareth liked to play, as he noted at the time. "I am blithely intuitive, at my best playing off the cuff and relying on instinct to make the right decision." By the time he retired he had also come to dislike the emphasis that was being placed by coaches on defence:

"Many players at the top level, particularly backs, are picked principally because of their defensive capabilities, their ability to tackle counting far more than their ability to get their line moving smoothly, to kick or pass well or to make a break. It is of genuine regret to me that in a game whose popularity and enjoyment has always been based upon flair and spontaneity, a missed tackle has become the most heinous crime on the rugby field and that one of the consequences of this is the creation of a negative approach amongst player which is alien to most of them... As a result we have dull, boring and entirely predictable action in most games at the top level."

A native of Tumble, Gareth, like Carwyn James, D. Ken Jones, Barry John and Jonathan Davies, was a product of Gwendraeth Grammar School and his talents were recognised while a pupil there by his selection for Wales Schoolboys and the Welsh Secondary Schools side. He had represented Tumble RFC at youth and senior level and while still only 17 years of age year he was selected for Carmarthenshire against North Wales and then against Monmouthshire in the Welsh Counties Cup final. In that game he scored two tries, a drop-goal and a penalty, a performance which he considers to be one of his best ever and which undoubtedly led to his being courted by Llanelli RFC where he served as an understudy to Phil Bennett for a short period. During that time he appeared five times for the club before he was 'poached' (in the opinion of some Scarlets supporters!) by Cardiff Rugby Club, where he remained for the rest of his playing career.

He joined the Black and Blues, at the instigation of Barry John, just after reaching his 18th birthday in November 1974. By this time Gareth was a student at the University of Wales Institute of Science and Technology in the city and the inconvenience of having to travel to west Wales to train and play was certainly instrumental in his decision to leave the Scarlets. Doubtless that the attraction of playing alongside Gareth Edwards for the Arms Park club was an additional enticement. However, the tardiness of the Llanelli club in granting him clearance

© Colorsport

to appear for his new club, which to many at the time smacked of sour grapes, meant that he did not make his debut for the first team until Boxing Day.

As well as representing Cardiff he was also required to turn out for the college team and in his second year he was part of the triumphant UWIST side that defeated

Swansea in the UAU final at Twickenham, thanks to his last-minute drop-goal. His student rugby achievements were further enhanced in 1977 when, having graduated in applied science at UWIST, he won a Blue at Oxford University, while studying for a teaching diploma. With Gareth in control the Dark Blues succeeded in defeating Cambridge for the first time in six years. Following his college days he continued to excel in the Cardiff team with the result that he was chosen to tour Australia with Wales in 1978, winning his first cap in the first Test in Brisbane, outside Brynmor Williams. In the next Test Gareth played alongside Terry Holmes, his scrum-half colleague at Cardiff, which was the beginning of a long and successful partnership in the Wales team. Until Gareth was forced to stand down because of injury, they played together for Wales in the next eight internationals and appeared together on eight further occasions over the next few years. In addition to their association on the field they and their families also became firm friends.

During the few years which followed his debut for Wales Gareth probably played his best rugby ever, particularly in the red jersey, and was an exceptionally gifted exponent of so many of the talents that are associated with stand-off play. He was a stylish, graceful runner, with none of the darting, staccato traits with which some fly-halves are associated, which seemed to complement a calm and unflustered temperament. His upright posture gave the impression that he was coasting along, with the option of shifting to higher a gear if required. He had an extremely safe pair of hands, with an ability to take passes thrown sometimes in unexpected directions. This skill was doubtless allied to his talents as a cricketer, another sport at which he excelled and at which he represented the Welsh Secondary Schools and Glamorgan Seconds. He was very adept at getting his three-quarter line moving smoothly and effectively and was a master at reading and controlling a game. Coupled with the aura of confidence that he regularly projected was a refusal to capitulate or to admit defeat, an admirable quality for someone playing in such an influential position.

In that connection perhaps his greatest attribute was his exceptional kicking ability. No other outside-half included in this collection could kick from the hand with such prodigious length while at the same time attaining such a degree of accuracy. With this particular talent, which as a young lad he nurtured religiously at the expense of other facets of fly-half play, he was often able to efficiently relieve pressure on his own team's defence whilst simultaneously pinning back the opposition to territories from which they would prefer not to operate. In the same way he could utilise such kicks for purely attacking purposes. In addition, he was an extremely able kicker of drop-goals and, particularly with Cardiff, a proficient place-kicker. He did, however, have one particular shortcoming. On his own admission he never liked to tackle and, given the opportunity, would shy away from undertaking such an onerous task!

His success with Cardiff and Wales led to his being selected for the British Lions to tour South Africa in 1980, which however turned out to be a disappointment for him. Having shown great promise in the opening provincial games, he received an injury which prevented him from being considered for the first Test. Nevertheless, he recovered in time to be selected for the second Test only to be carried off following a tackle by Naas Botha, which kept him out of rugby for six months. Consequently he suffered the disappointment, along with Terry Holmes and two other badly injured players, of having to return home early, having played in only four matches.

He next appeared for Wales in the autumn and in the first two games of the Five Nations. However, following a poor display against Scotland at Murrayfield he was dropped for the two remaining internationals that season. He returned as captain to face Australia in December 1981 and retained his place for the Five Nations games in 1982 of which only one resulted in a Welsh victory. After the final game, when Wales were trounced by Scotland at the Arms Park, six players were dropped never to play for their country again. Gareth's performances, in the opinion of the critics, had been disappointing and his attitude was considered to have been *too* casual and laid-back. By the following season John Bevan had been appointed coach of the Wales team and Gareth was ignored for the next ten games, during which period Malcolm Dacey was the preferred choice at outside-half. Davies attributes this to the fact that he and Bevan did not get on and that consequently he wasn't a popular selection with the coach. Owing to injuries to other leading outside-halves, Gareth was recalled to the Wales team for the first three games of the Five Nations Championship in 1985.

He later admitted that he took no pleasure in playing for his country during this particular period, mainly because, as noted above, under the Bevan formula he was given no latitude to call the shots, a duty which he considered to be inherent in basic outside-half play and which he so enjoyed performing with Cardiff. Indeed during 1983–4 he had created a club record by scoring 338 points, which he broke the following season with a total of 365 points. For the last game of the 1985 Five Nations the selectors uncharacteristically announced the team nine days before the match, and selected A.N. Other in the fly-half position. Two days later Gareth Davies and Malcolm Dacey were expected to be in direct opposition in a club match between Swansea and Cardiff, after which the selectors would seemingly choose between them for the number ten spot. To Gareth, the implication of such action was that they no longer had confidence in him as the incumbent outside-half in the Wales team. His disappointment and anger was exacerbated by the fact that he heard of the selectors' plans via a third party and not directly from a WRU official.

In the light of such developments Gareth, having won 22 caps for his country, informed the selectors that he no longer wished to be considered for the Wales team and consequently won many admirers for the dignified manner in which he had responded to the recent developments. He had a good game against Swansea, outplaying his rival, and the selectors chose Jonathan Davies to play his first game for Wales against England. At the end of that season Gareth also retired from club rugby, having had eleven illustrious seasons with Cardiff, creating a club record for an aggregate of 2,753 points, in 326 matches, comprising 71 tries, 567 conversions, 54 drop-goals and 291 penalties. For Wales he scored 46 points, including nine drop-goals, but his one big regret was that he had never scored a try in the Wales jersey. In 1982 he was offered an opportunity to play for Natal and Western Province, with lucrative job offers forming part of the contracts in question and, similarly, Toulon Rugby Club tried to tempt him in 1984, but all to no avail. His other honours as a player included many appearances at home and abroad for the Barbarians, for whom he became a selector on his retirement in 1985.

His career off the field of play has been particularly successful with a number of influential appointments which were to benefit significantly from his extensive business and managerial acumen. While still playing he held positions with firstly the Burnley Building Society and then the Northern and Provincial Building Society. Upon his retirement as a player he became assistant director of the CBI in Wales and then in 1989 he was appointed head of sport for BBC Wales. Although he had little experience of broadcasting he was extremely influential in procuring substantial contracts and in the development and expansion of the Corporations sporting provisions in Wales. Other important positions followed, namely chief executive of Cardiff Athletic Club, chairman of the Sports Council for Wales, commissioning editor for sports and events with S4C, director of Welsh affairs for the Royal Mail, and head of International Business Wales in Australia, based in Sydney, for the Welsh Assembly Government. Following a number of years as dean of the Carnegie Faculty of Sport and Education at the Leeds Metropolitan University, he was recently appointed as chief executive of Newport Gwent Dragons.

GLYN DAVIES

Accoording to Cliff Morgan, writing in 2002, Glyn Davies was "probably the most naturally gifted player that I remember at outside-half... he had more fly-half talent in his little finger than any other of his time had in their whole frame... if I wanted to be like anybody, it was Glyn." Glyn Davies first played for Wales in the Victory Internationals of 1946 while still a student at Pontypridd County School. He had excelled in a school team which had become renowned for playing scintillating rugby and had lost just three games in five years. For much of that time he was the architect of its success. He was a native of Cilfynydd, a village which, of course, became associated with an international star in other fields, Sir Geraint Evans, who married Glyn's sister, Brenda.

Glyn started his senior rugby career with Cilfynydd but, although he turned out in four games for Cardiff in 1946, his immediate future lay with the Pontypridd club where he spent many hours being schooled in the arts of half-back play by the groundsman Dick Cotes. It was from there that he was first capped, as a 19 year old in 1947 while doing National Service. In 1948 he enrolled at St Catherine's College, Cambridge and was later awarded his Blue, a feat which he also achieved in the following two years, in addition to being made captain of the university rugby team during his final year. In 1950, owing to an injury suffered by the Newport outside-half Roy Burnett, he played some twelve games for the Gwent club before finishing his career with Clifton and then Bristol.

As defined in the Introduction by the author Alun Richards (one of his contemporaries in that victorious Pontypridd County School team) Glyn Davies was undoubtedly a 'High Church' fly-half. Not being particularly renowned for physical play, being just 5' 9" tall and weighing 11 stone, or for his defensive exploits, he was above all an attacking player who could enthral spectators with the poise and grace with which he would beat defenders. He possessed commendable handling skills coupled with a clinical ability to sidestep off either foot. The frequent addition of a subtle change of pace often supplemented his footballing skills and his talent for beating defenders with hip-swaying elegance also gave his three-quarter line scope to capitalise on the space which he created. In true High Church tradition, he succeeded in implementing such attributes with a seemingly effortless ease which bordered on arrogance, all of which gave the impression of his being able to do so with plenty of time to spare.

Until 1950 the Wales players wore letters, as opposed to numbers, on the back of their shirts, therefore when Glyn Davies donned his first Welsh jersey as an outside-half against Scotland in 1947, he bore the letter F. Yet by the time he played his last game for Wales in 1951, the practice of having numbered jerseys had been introduced which meant that as a fly-half he had number 6 on his back. That first game against Scotland, which resulted in a 22–8 victory for Wales, was a telling indication of Glyn's ability to utilise his backs effectively, in that each member of his three-quarter line crossed for tries on that day.

It was initially thought that, since he was just a teenager when he won his first cap against Scotland in Cardiff in 1947, he had cemented his place in the Welsh line-up for years to come. However, having been forced to miss the next game through injury, he spent most of the following seasons vying with Billy Cleaver for the fly-half position. During the next few years it appeared that for the anticipated closely-fought matches Billy was favoured by the selectors, whereas Glyn was their choice if it seemed that a particular encounter was likely to produce more free-flowing rugby. Some notable performances by Glyn, for example at St Helen's in 1951, when he splendidly orchestrated a five-try rout of England, were tempered with disappointing displays, such as the 1949 and 1951 fixtures at Murrayfield when he was mercilessly hounded by the Scottish back row. He did not feature at all in the Wales team that won the Grand Slam in 1950. Indeed during that latter Murrayfield fixture noted above, he suffered the ignominy of being switched from fly-half to centre by the captain, John Gwilliam, because "he'd had one big bump too many", a move considered by many at the time to be particularly demoralising for the team. Wales lost the game by 19–0, which came to be known for some time as the 'Murrayfield Massacre'. Glyn, at the age of 23, was consequently dropped, never to play for Wales again and having won eleven caps. He was replaced for the Ireland match by a new star on the horizon, Cliff Morgan, and the confusion which prevailed amongst Welsh rugby officials at the time was perhaps illustrated by the fact that when the team to play that particular match was announced it contained five renowned players bearing the same name, namely A.N. Other!

It was a source of considerable amazement to many rugby pundits at the time that a player who had displayed so much talent and such promise as Glyn Davies could be discarded by the national selectors despite the fact that he still had many years of rugby to come. That he had been heralded on his arrival on the international scene just four years earlier as the harbinger of a new dawn in Welsh back play made his dismissal even more difficult to fathom. It is true, however, that the very essence of his game, in his quest for inventiveness and flair, would leave him exposed to frailties on which predatory back rows thrived. For, according to the laws of the game which prevailed at the time, wing-forwards were allowed to break early from set pieces and eagerly await their opportunity to devour their fly-half prey, who stood but a few yards away. In such circumstances his efforts to be creative could sometimes be well and truly thwarted. At the end of his rugby-playing days Glyn Davies settled in France and established himself as a successful businessman in the wine trade. He died in Bristol in 1976 at the comparatively young age of 49.

JONATHAN DAVIES

H E WAS DESCRIBED by Jacques Fouroux, the former France scrum-half and captain, who was the French team coach during Jonathan's tenure as the Wales outside-half, as 'the Maradona of rugby union'. Stephen Jones, the respected *Sunday Times* rugby journalist, at about the same time, when referring to Jonathan's place in the famous Welsh fly-half hierarchy, described him as 'unquestionably the greatest of all, the richest and the complete talent. His single greatest failing is that he was born at the wrong time'. In that respect he echoed the sentiments of Clem Thomas, the celebrated Wales and British Lions flanker. "He played behind the worst (Welsh) pack in living memory, and when you achieve what he achieved under those circumstances, you must be a great player... He worked miracles..." Another notable Welsh rugby forward, Brian Thomas, who won 21 caps for his country and who was Jonathan's team manager at Neath Rugby Club, described him as the best outside-half he had ever seen.

Despite such glowing accolades his fly-half talents were recognised at a much later stage in his career than those of his predecessors playing in that position for Wales. For example, he never won schoolboy, secondary school or youth international honours. As well as playing for the school team, he regularly turned out for his village team, Trimsaran Youth, with whom he had particularly strong ties. He had never been academically inclined and had not been greatly inspired by his sixth-form studies. At the age of 17 he left school to take up an apprenticeship as a painter and decorator, while his passion for rugby was satisfied by playing for Trimsaran Youth. Nonetheless, it was his ambition to eventually join a first-class club, preferably Llanelli, so in 1981, at the age of 18, he asked the club for a pre-season trial. Although he thought he had played quite well he received, much to his disappointment, no reaction at all from the coaches who were present and subsequently heard nothing from the club. He described how his consequent despondency was exacerbated by a realisation that "I had fallen a long way behind my ambitions. Rugby is such an intense part of life in the area, that to have reached the age of 18 without some major recognition of your ability is to be virtually wiped out as a big-time prospect."

From a very young age great things had been expected of Jonathan, known as 'Jiffy' to his friends for no apparent reason. As a nine year old playing in an Under 11 seven-a-side competition he was chosen by Carwyn James as the player of the tournament. He was so impressed by his performance that he asked the organisers if Jonathan could keep the winner's trophy on the understanding that he, Carwyn, would buy a new one for the following year's competition. He saw Jonathan play again two years later and told him that one day he would play for Wales. At that time the Trimsaran Primary School pupil was greatly influenced by his teacher, Meirion Davies, a former hooker with London Welsh, Cardiff and Llanelli, whose basic philosophy of running and passing the ball as much as possible, with kicking being a last resort, ideally pandered to Jonathan's natural inclinations to play open,

© Getty Images

adventurous rugby and to his innate confidence to try the unexpected, even at that tender age.

Following the fruitless trial with Llanelli, he was advised by Meirion, who was by now coaching at Trimsaran Rugby Club, to immerse himself in playing for the senior team there. The tough and often rugged nature of their matches, and specific efforts on Jonathan's part to improve his speed and strength, nurtured a physicality which suitably complemented his abundant natural skills. In due course he made his mark at that particular level and at the apparent instigation of Phil Bennett, he received an invitation from Neath RFC, who were having difficulties in finding a fly-half who merited selection on a regular basis, to turn out for them against Pontypridd on a cold Tuesday evening in February 1982. For the 19 year old it was the birth of a first-class rugby career which was to earn him worldwide recognition.

He had an excellent game and was made Man of the Match by no less a personage than John Dawes. He played a few more games for Neath before the end of the season, while still registered with Trimsaran. For it was his wish to remain for the time being with his village club as he was favourite to be selected for the outside-half berth in the Welsh Districts team. Since he had never won international recognition at any level he hoped to earn a cap at Districts Level if not any other – a feat which he achieved later that season.

Having signed for Neath during the summer, he turned out for them at the annual Welsh Snelling Sevens tournament and suffered a ligament injury which kept him sidelined for 18 months. Then, following just one game for the reserve team, and despite his protestations to the team manager, Brian Thomas, he was selected in 1984 for Neath against Newport in a Welsh Cup quarter-final. Once again he won the Man of the Match award, following a memorable performance which led to a personal tally of 19 points. This was the beginning of an amazingly successful four-year period as the Neath fly-half, during which he was diligently and prudently mentored by Thomas, who was soon to describe his prodigy as "a Barry John who could tackle"! At the age of 22 Jonathan became the youngest captain in the club's history and inspired the team to reach great heights. For a number of seasons he was the linchpin not only of the best team in Wales but also, by virtue of Neath's comprehensive defeat of Bath, the ruling champions of England in 1987, of effectively the best team in Britain. The attractive and successful rugby played at the Gnoll inevitably drew supporters in large numbers, yet it was said at the time that Jonathan alone would be responsible for increasing attendance by 40 per cent when he appeared.

Playing behind an all-conquering pack he relished the opportunities they provided to enable him to display his abundant talents. He revelled in running at opponents with the ball in hand and leaving them in his wake as a result of devastating speed off the mark, or a clinically deceptive change of pace, or a scintillating sidestep or an astutely judged grubber or chip kick, or perhaps a combination of two or more of these attributes, thus making him one of the most exciting players in world rugby. His game was built on a total reliance on instinct and he summed up his appetite for trying the seemingly impossible as follows: "Sometimes I've set off even before I am sure myself where I am headed for. It is a most exciting feeling and I get as much thrill as the crowd do because it is as much of a surprise to me that I've found a gap as it is to them... Many have talked about my speed off the mark but they neglect to take into account that the fastest thing off the mark is my brain." One of the additional requirements of a successful outside-half was the ability to read the manner in which a game was developing on the field and to dictate the play accordingly. Jonathan was a 'natural' in that respect and assumed such responsibility with ease. Coupled with this particular aspect of his game was the confidence and apparent cockiness he displayed when strutting his skills. To his critics this would often border on arrogance, while his supporters would claim that it was simply the manifestation of Jonathan's joy and exuberance at being given the opportunity to display his talents on such a personally rewarding stage.

Jonathan's success with Neath was recognised in the 1984–5 season at the national level. Having played firstly for Wales B, and having won a place on the bench for the Wales game against France he was selected, after playing in 35 first-class rugby matches, for his country's last game of the Five Nations Championship against England at Cardiff, to win the first of 32 caps. The visitors were beaten 24–15 with Jonathan making a considerable contribution to the victory, scoring a try and a drop-goal. He continued to impress with his enterprising and often sparkling displays for the next few seasons despite the Wales forwards' failure to provide a satisfactory supply of the ball for the three-quarters. During the Five Nations Championship in 1986 Wales won but two games and were victorious in only one game in the following season's competition.

By this time Jonathan was in demand worldwide as an outstanding seven-a-side player, a game which was ideally suited to his particular talents. Rugby league clubs began to show great interest and he was offered £100,000 by Leeds to go North, something which he admitted in the press he would probably consider in the future. Indeed that particular development echoed his father's rugby career, who, as a talented centre with Swansea and Llanelli, at one stage considered an offer from Leigh Rugby League Club. He had been a great inspiration to his son during his childhood but sadly died from a long illness when Jonathan was 14 years old.

In the light of press speculation about the possibility

of Jonathan leaving rugby union, Brian Thomas sought a commitment from him as to his future with Neath, which Jonathan was not prepared to give. The result, much to his surprise, was a rather contentious statement from the club at the end of the 1987 season that he would no longer be part of Neath's future plans. Within a month he was representing Wales at the inaugural World Cup in New Zealand and was instrumental in securing an unexpected third place position for his country, who had previously been defeated in the semi-final against the All Blacks.

On his return home Jonathan joined Llanelli and, after missing the start of the following season due to injury, proceeded to play perhaps his best rugby for his country in the 1988 Five Nations Championship, during which Wales won the Triple Crown. Following his sparkling performance at Twickenham he went on to score one of the best tries of his international career against Scotland. Having skilfully taken a hurried, looping pass from his scrum-half, Robert Jones, from whom he received an impeccable service in all but four of his international appearances, he sidestepped Calder, the on-rushing Scotland flanker, cleverly kicked the ball past the covering number eight, White, and scorched through to touch down.

Great things were then expected from the Wales tour to New Zealand the following May, which turned out to be a disaster. Both Tests resulted in heavy defeats, the second of which, nonetheless, saw Jonathan heroically skipper the side and also score a memorable try following a 90-yard run for the line. Although his team was comprehensively beaten Jonathan was made Man of the Match. In New Zealand Wales had also been outclassed in many of the provincial matches and, despite his own commendable performances, which featured particularly committed and resolute defensive displays on his part, Jonathan returned home completely disillusioned. Unsatisfactory hotel arrangements, an unacceptable travel itinerary and a hectic playing schedule compounded the touring party's grievances, yet Jonathan's request, upon his return home, to address the WRU regarding his concerns was completely ignored. His playing achievements were however widely recognised by his being chosen as the Whitbread Rugby World Player of the Year in 1988.

He became increasingly aggrieved at the indifferent manner in which the Wales players were treated at international level and at the lack of security for them and their families afforded by their rugby careers. In New Zealand, for example, he witnessed the ways in which the careers of the All Blacks were comfortably cushioned by corporate inducements, endorsements and sponsorships which enabled them to concentrate entirely on rugby matters. The IRB rules as applied by the WRU entertained no such provisions and its management showed no interest in addressing the problem. In addition, the autumn saw Wales, skippered by Jonathan, being defeated by the unfancied Romanian team which led to some criticism of his leadership and a somewhat lacklustre individual performance, which served as a catalyst for his decision to join Widnes Rugby League Club, for a reputed record of £225,000 in January 1989, at the age of 26. Some weeks later when the BBC asked the WRU for permission to interview him at the Arms Park before the Wales–England game the request was refused.

Despite his irrefutable achievements as a union player,

it is commonly believed that he played his best rugby whilst with Widnes, for whom he scored 1,184 points, and later Warrington, where he notched up over 600 points. Having overcome some initial problems at Widnes, a period which he later described as the most difficult in his rugby career, he developed to become one of the greatest utility backs ever to play the game. A combination of outstanding attacking and defensive skills, the latter having been boosted by a deliberate effort to put on weight, saw him gradually adapt to the ferocious physicality of rugby league, contrary to the expectations of numerous pundits. In due course he won almost every possible honour with Widnes and also made eleven appearances for Great Britain between 1990–4, which included one of the most memorable tries ever scored at Wembley in the defeat of the world champions, Australia in 1994. He appeared nine times for Wales, leading them to the semi-final of the Rugby League World Cup, and toured New Zealand with the Lions in 1990. He was named Player of the Season by his fellow professionals on two occasions winning also the supreme accolade of Man of Steel. In addition to making his mark in English rugby league, he excelled 'down under' when spending two summers playing in the extremely physical Australian League.

In 1996, as his wife Karen was sadly suffering from a terminal illness, Jonathan expressed a wish to come back to Wales. A relaxation of IRB rules allowed players who had gone North to return to play for union clubs. In that connection, Gareth Davies, who was now the chief executive of Cardiff Rugby Club, engineered a deal between Jewsons, two millionaire businessmen, BBC Wales and the WRU to enable Jonathan to join the Arms

Park club. His early appearances for Cardiff were in the full-back position and were thought to have been initially tainted, for whatever petty reasons, by a shameful decision by his fellow players to deliberately avoid passing the ball to him. He still possessed a number of the skills that Welsh crowds had witnessed years before but the trademark burst of speed had now disappeared. He was selected as outside-half for Wales on two further occasions and made two other brief appearances in the centre as a replacement off the bench.

He was awarded the MBE in 1996 and the following year he was being mentioned as a possible contender for a place on the Lions tour to South Africa. However, after the tragic death of his wife, he retired from the game in order that he might devote more time to his three young children. In recent years he has become one of the most respected TV analysts of both rugby union and rugby league. He is a past president of the Crusaders, the Welsh Super Rugby League club and regularly hosts a chat show bearing his name on S4C. He married his second wife, Helen, in 2002.

DAVID EVANS

B ORN IN WOOTTON Bassett in 1965, David Evans was educated at Aberdare Comprehensive School. He represented Wales in rugby at a variety of levels before winning his first cap for the senior team in the centre against France at Parc des Princes in 1989. He had captained the Welsh Secondary Schools side and appeared for Welsh Students, Welsh Universities, Wales A and Wales B. Having attended UCW Swansea from where he graduated in management science, he studied at St Anne's College, Oxford and obtained a postgraduate diploma in social studies. While a student there he won a rugby Blue and in that particular match against Cambridge he opposed Mike Hall, who played alongside him two months later in David's first game for Wales in Paris. David also toured Fiji, Australia and New Zealand with the Oxbridge side.

He was a creative and intelligent player whose deceptive running was a joy to watch and a problem for defenders. His time in the Wales team unfortunately coincided with a particularly disappointing series of performances by the national side. On the twelve occasions that he represented Wales (four of which were as a replacement) he appeared on the winning side just twice with the team conceding 137 points in the first five games that he played for his country. Having been selected at centre for his first three games he then appeared regularly at outside-half in 1990, winning five caps. He made three appearances as a substitute in 1991 (two of which were in World Cup Pool matches) and remarkably did not appear again on the international stage until he took to the field as a replacement outside-half against Japan in the first Pool game of the 1995 World Cup in South Africa, by which time he was playing with Treorchy.

While at UCW Swansea, whom he represented at the UAU final at Twickenham in 1988, he also played for Cardiff Rugby Club. He joined the Black and Blues, having turned out previously for Aberaman, as a 19 year old in 1984 and in the 117 games that he played for the Arms Park club, over a period of seven seasons, he amassed a total of 667 points, comprising 29 tries, 121 conversions, 99 penalties and four drop-goals. In 1991 he left Cardiff to play for Treorchy and won the last of his twelve caps while with the Rhondda club.

After leaving Oxford David became a finance representative with Chartered Trust PLC, a position he held for two years. Then, for a period of 17 years he was high performance manager with Sport Wales before being employed, since 2008, as international sports event manager by the Welsh Government.

CARWYN JAMES

C ARWYN JAMES AND Barry John had remarkably similar
backgrounds. Apart from becoming extremely
talented outside-halves at the highest level, both were raised
in the west Wales village of Cefneithin and were sons of
coal miners. Both had a great interest in soccer and were
offered trials in their youth by professional clubs, Cardiff
City in the case of Carwyn while Barry was approached
by Coventry City. Their early interest in rugby was
stimulated by the accomplishments of players on the local
rugby field and both became central to the achievements
of the Gwendraeth Grammar School rugby team. The two
were ardent supporters of the Scarlets and, having already
turned out for the Cefneithin senior team, both appeared
for Llanelli while still at school. Both, when in their prime,
turned down offers to join leading rugby league clubs. In
addition to possessing the essential practical skills needed
in their position, they were both endowed with the ability
to manage efficiently proceedings on the field of play and
with a knack of analysing effectively, for the benefit of the
team, the performance of the opposition. Both had the
same basic philosophy with regard to the essence of rugby,
namely that it was a game to be enjoyed and that instinct
and flair were attributes which were to be encouraged at
all times.

There were, of course, many differences between the
two. Carwyn won six caps with the Wales Secondary
Schools team, an honour which eluded Barry. The former

achieved greater renown as a coach than as a player, while the latter never ventured into that field following his retirement. However, by virtue of the fact that he belonged to a slightly younger generation, Barry had the great fortune of being able to adopt Carwyn as his role model, during his own development as a fly-half, while his hero delighted Stradey followers of the 1950s with his entertaining and accomplished play.

Having played a few matches for Llanelli as a 17 year old, Carwyn's enthusiasm and confidence was literally shaken in a game against Neath at the Gnoll when he was late-tackled rather solidly by Leighton Davies, the sturdy home centre. As a result Carwyn, apart from a few isolated appearances for the Stradey club, was happy enough, during the next four years, to play for UCW Aberystwyth, where he had enrolled in 1948 to pursue an honours degree in Welsh. It took him a while to earn his place in the College First XV during which time he turned out for the Seconds and also for Aberystwyth Town. While in his first year he also played occasionally for Amman United in the West Wales League, since his home club, Cefneithin, was not to receive full WRU status until that particular season. Upon his graduation Carwyn undertook a compulsory period of National Service, which he spent, as a member of the Navy, at the Joint Services School for Linguistics in Surrey, where he studied Russian. He later took pleasure in the irony of the fact that he spent two years in the Navy without ever seeing a boat! He did, however, represent the Navy at rugby and often turned out for Devonport Services, who at that time had regular fixtures against first-class clubs. However, his main delight in those days was to play for

London Welsh, whom he also captained in a victorious campaign at the Middlesex Sevens.

In 1954 he returned to west Wales and obtained a post as a teacher at Queen Elizabeth Grammar School, Carmarthen. As part of their pre-season preparations Swansea Rugby Club invited Carwyn to go a tour to Romania that year, an experience which he greatly enjoyed. In the light of the Whites' interest in acquiring his services, Llanelli made determined and eventually successful efforts to sign him. He played at Stradey until 1960, when he decided to return, for his final season as a player, to Cefneithin. As captain he led the village team during the most successful season in its history, as they won both the West Wales League Championship and Cup, an achievement which Carwyn described in later years, with all sincerity, as being as important to him as any other honour in his rugby career. Carwyn also welcomed opportunities to engage in two other sporting activities from which he took great pleasure, namely snooker and cricket. He was also a keen supporter of Glamorgan Cricket Club and would admit that, had he been sufficiently talented, he would have loved to have been a professional cricketer.

For six seasons at Stradey Carwyn had regularly displayed his prolific talents as a fly-half. He was an elegant, balanced runner who excelled at deceiving and defying his opponents with breath-taking sidesteps, mystifying dummies and an uncanny capacity for exploiting any weakness in the opposition's play. His distribution and his handling were of the highest quality but perhaps the most appealing facet of his game was his desire to play attacking, entertaining and open rugby whenever possible. Notwithstanding this basic credo, which was to form such an important aspect of his coaching career, his abilities as a tactical kicker and as a drop-goal specialist were widely acclaimed.

While a player with Llanelli he appeared in several Welsh trials but had the misfortune to be a contemporary of the brilliant Cliff Morgan. In the opinion of many at the time Carwyn would sometimes outshine the incumbent Wales outside-half in such trial matches but the selectors seemed always to favour the Cardiff player. Carwyn was finally rewarded with his first cap against Australia in 1958 following Morgan's withdrawal through injury. He played very well as Wales won by 9–3, clinching the victory with a 40-yard drop-goal, having already played an important part in a try scored by winger John Collins. Nevertheless he was omitted from the team for the next match against England at Twickenham in order to accommodate the fit-again Cliff Morgan.

Carwyn rejoined him in the Wales team for the final international match of the season against France at the Arms Park, this time as a centre, in place of club-mate Cyril Davies. There were many who considered that playing Carwyn in that position did no justice to his natural talents as an outside half. However this was not the first time that he and Cliff had lined up together in those positions. The previous season both had turned out for a Welsh XV against an International XV (containing such stars as Tony O'Reilly, Jeff Butterfield and Arthur Smith) in a match to raise money for the Commonwealth Games to be held in Cardiff that year. The Welsh team were victorious by 17–16 and during that game Cliff and Carwyn sometimes interchanged positions. It was thought that when the Welsh side was announced for the France game that such a tactic would pay dividends but it was not to be. A defeat by 6–16 and a disappointing team performance saw both Carwyn and Cliff Morgan wear the red shirt for the last time.

That same year Carwyn was appointed as the first Welsh master at Llandovery College. He was still playing outside-half for Llanelli but within a few years, inspired in the main by the chief rugby coach at the college, T.P. Williams, he had started to develop an interest in coaching. In due course Carwyn succeeded T.P. as the First XV coach and soon stamped his unique perspective on the style of play adopted by the team. For example, for one season he banned the players from kicking the ball under all but the most desperate circumstances. In 1967, having attended formal coaching courses over the years, he was invited to take charge of the West Wales XV against the All Blacks at the start of their 1967 tour. Despite losing by 21–14 the home team and their coach had made a great impression and, not for the last time, the New Zealand team had cause to fear Carwyn's talents as a coach.

In 1969 he was appointed coach of the Llanelli team and pundits soon noticed that the Scarlets were playing the game in a similar vein to that advocated by Carwyn when he was at Llandovery. Even though there were obvious differences between the two levels, his basic philosophy was the same, namely that players should always feel free to express themselves on the field and that their priority should be to play attacking, creative rugby whenever possible. At that particular stage in his career his teaching and pastoral duties at Llandovery often clashed with the ever increasing demands upon him as a club coach. As a result he obtained a post as a lecturer in Welsh at Trinity

College, Carmarthen, where the academic life offered him greater freedom.

However that was only a partial justification for his new appointment. For Carwyn had an unbridled love of Welsh literature and the Welsh language. He was captivated by the works of particular poets and prose writers, had much regard for the classics and literature in general and took pleasure from meaningful literary discussion. He was a fluent Russian speaker and had a great regard for the works of leading Russian playwrights. While still playing for Llanelli he spent one summer vacation at the National Library researching the works of one of the *cywyddwyr* (a Welsh strict-metre poet) of the Middle Ages. He became a frequent contributor to radio and television literary programmes and was also an ardent supporter of the activities of the National Eisteddfod. He was also an active member of Plaid Cymru, standing as a parliamentary candidate in the Labour stronghold of Llanelli in 1970 and had been a deacon and secretary at his beloved Tabernacle Chapel in Cefneithin since 1955. The academic nature of his new calling and the opportunity to convey to prospective teachers the infectious enthusiasm which he brought to his wide range of interests meant that he found his five years at Carmarthen to be extremely rewarding.

Having coached the Scarlets to within a whisker of defeating the Springboks in 1970, Carwyn chose not to watch the match as a personal protest against the apartheid regime that was still in force in South Africa (he did however accept invitations to visit the country in later years, prior to the downfall of that regime). However, that particular game served to enhance his reputation as a coach and in 1971 he was invited to apply for the post of coach and assistant manager to the British Lions on their tour of New Zealand. He was asked by the interviewing panel, in view of his Plaid Cymru beliefs, whether it was safe to appoint a 'narrow minded Nationalist' to such an important position. Carwyn's reply apparently enlightened the panel as to how a Nationalist could also be an enthusiastic Internationalist.

Similarly, having secured the appointment, in his initial talk to the Lions tour party at Eastbourne prior to their departure, he addressed the fact that some critics saw the selection of a fairly large contingent of Welsh players as a problem. Carwyn explained that, for some of the party, Welsh was their mother tongue, as it was for him, and he would be communicating with them in that language. He would use English when it was deemed appropriate and the English-speaking majority should not think that when he turned to Welsh he was speaking in code in order to pass disparaging remarks about the non-Welsh speakers! That frank declaration served to set the tone for a tour which saw Carwyn gain the unequivocal support and admiration of the entire party.

Their historic achievement in winning that Test series was masterminded by Carwyn. His preparation for every tour game was meticulous and his prowess as a shrewd tactician was second to none. It is said that he had chosen his teams, injuries permitting, for the first seven games in New Zealand before the Lions had left Britain, and that, even at that stage, he was fairly certain of the composition of the team for the first Test. Notwithstanding his inclinations to that end, his mastery of the prospective minefield of man-management was admirable. The success of the tour was in no small way due to his charismatic approach and his unique way of communicating individually with players, in order to encourage them to believe in themselves and in their ability to compete for a place in the Test team. The respectful, perceptive and non-dogmatic manner in which he conducted his training sessions entailed that the morale of the party was always at the highest level, as was the esteem in which he was held by all during the tour. His genial personality and the courtesy which he afforded all who approached him, regardless of the painful skin ailment which often made life uncomfortable for him, won him many admirers. In recognition of his achievements in New Zealand he was awarded the OBE in 1972 but felt obliged to politely decline the honour.

In 1974 he was invited to make an application for the post of Welsh national team coach, but decided not to accept the invitation. He was strongly opposed to the practice of five laymen being responsible for choosing the Welsh team. Therefore, in a letter to the WRU he assumed that his request that the new coach should be chairman of the Welsh selectors, with three advisors (preferably regional coaches) to assist him with the team selection, would be refused, so he was not prepared to be considered for the post. He did not receive a reply from the WRU. He continued as coach of the Llanelli team and, as a result of his enlightened and meticulous preparations, saw his team gain a historic victory against the visiting All Blacks in 1972. He was also instrumental in their winning the Welsh Cup on four occasions between 1973–6.

The demands upon him on his return from New Zealand had been immense and, in due course, he felt that he would be best suited to meet those demands if he left the disciplined academic life for the apparent freedom of a career as a broadcaster (and later as a journalist in addition), a change which he undertook in 1974. Paradoxically, despite the excellence of his media pursuits and despite the supreme efficiency of his work as a rugby coach, Carwyn was often notoriously ill-disciplined in managing his personal affairs. For example mail was often left unopened for long periods and public speaking engagements would sometimes be accepted from two widespread locations on the same evening!

The pressures of broadcasting led him, in 1977, to seek a complete break from it all and to accept an invitation to spend two years in Tuscany as coach to the Rovigo club. As well as winning many friends with his customary charm and pleasant personality, his inspirational leadership took the team to their first Italian Championship. He also availed himself of the opportunity to be immersed in Italian culture and to learn the native language. He took advantage of many opportunities to integrate with the local community, for example it is said that, having been invited to address the sixth-form English class at the local grammar school, he captivated the students there with his views on romanticism in literature.

In January 1983 Carwyn James, at the age of 53, died of a heart attack at his hotel in Amsterdam while on a short vacation. His funeral in Cefneithin was attended by several hundred people, from all walks of life, including representatives of the rugby world from far and wide, all of whom had come to mourn and to honour a special person, player and coach, for whom there was always the utmost respect.

NEIL JENKINS

A s HAS BEEN already noted, for many years, particularly during the 1980s and 1990s, it seemed that the basic remedy adopted by the Wales selectors to cure a bad performance by the national team was to change the outside-half for the next game. The underlying causes of such poor displays were often ignored, with the result that an incoming outside-half selected to offset the difficulties experienced by the team was frequently subjected to the same fundamental flaws, in particular a paucity of quality possession from the forwards which often entailed that the fly-half had to play much of his game on the back foot.

The fact that Neil Jenkins was considered to be one of the best ever goal-kickers in Test match rugby and that he became one of the most efficient distributors ever to play for Wales (he was described by his contemporary, Ieuan Evans, as the best passer of the ball he had ever seen) was lost on some. As indeed was the fact that it was only his prodigious goal-kicking record that managed to sustain many mediocre Wales performances during his tenure in the national team. Yet in his early games in the red shirt he was not included for his kicking prowess (those duties fell to Paul Thorburn) but purely as a running, linking outside-half.

He was born into a rugby orientated family, with his father and two of his uncles being particularly instrumental in nurturing his early interest and development in the game. He played for Llantwit Fardre Youth at just 14 years old before joining the Pontypridd Rugby Club Youth XV. At that time he was particularly fast, often playing on the wing and it was in that position he was selected, at the age of 16, for the WRU President's Youth XV. Following that game he was invited to attend a residential training course at Aberystwyth which served as a preparatory school for the Welsh Youth team. Neil found the town boring and left after a week, yet this did not prevent him from being selected in due course to represent Wales Youth against the Welsh Colleges, Italy and then England, a game which saw him score all of his country's points in a notable 12–6 victory.

After four years of rugby at youth level he made his debut for the Pontypridd senior side in April 1990. From that point onward his ascendancy to senior international rugby was rapid. Within two months of that debut he was chosen for the WRU President's Select Under 21 team to face an All Blacks Under 21 XV, which was followed a month later by an appearance for the Wales B team. After just 15 games for Pontypridd he won his first senior cap against England at Cardiff at the age of 19 years old, along with Scott Gibbs, one year after both had played for Wales against the same opponents at youth level. Neil retained his place for the remainder of the 1991 Five Nations tournament but, despite being a member of the Wales party on the disastrous tour to Australia that summer, he was not included in the World Cup squad later that year.

He next appeared for his country in the 1992 Five Nations tournament, playing the first three games in the centre before reverting to outside-half for the final game against Scotland. Between his debut as fly-half in January 1991 and his recall in March 1992, Wales had also played

Adrian Davies, Mark Ring and Colin Stephens in that position! Wales didn't score against England in the 1992 Championship but in the three remaining games Neil kicked nine penalties and one conversion. That season, with particular regard to the manner in which he was required to alternate between various positions and to the significant contribution he made to the team's points tally, was indicative of the general pattern of his early career with Wales.

For when he was selected as outside-half for the 18th time in 1993–4 it was his fourth stint in that position. In all he was dropped as fly-half on seven occasions but had the versatility to merit his inclusion in the team as centre and full-back on other occasions. Fellow fly-halves, such as Barry John, Phil Bennett, Gareth Davies and Jonathan Davies, had also suffered a similar fate at some stage in their careers but Neil Jenkins was perhaps more maligned than his illustrious predecessors. For he not only had to suffer the incongruities of the Wales selectors but also the general disenchantment of many rugby followers and sometimes hostile media, who had erroneously expected him to claim his place in the sidestepping, jinking lineage of previous incumbents.

In many ways he was a product of the changing climate in world rugby at the time. Players had become faster and fitter, with the result that there was less space for an adventurous fly-half to display any attacking flair that he might possess. A greater emphasis on defensive skills and retaining possession and a significant dependence on 'risk-free' rugby meant that players, especially outside-halves, were not so inclined to undertake individual sorties or to indulge in expansive rugby in the face of increasingly

flat and linear-organised defences. In this respect the game had become more suited to the particular talents that Neil Jenkins possessed which led to his being considered by many to be the forerunner of the modern breed of fly-half.

After ten very successful years with Pontypridd, during which the club won the Welsh Cup and also, under Neil's captaincy, the Welsh Championship, he joined Cardiff Rugby Club in November 1999. He returned briefly to Sardis Road in 2002–3 before joining the Celtic Warriors during their brief period as one of the professional regional sides in Wales. In 237 appearances for Pontypridd, with whom he established a lifelong bond, he scored a record 3,185 points. He was a particular favourite with the supporters there who were perhaps more fortunate than his followers at international matches in that he was frequently allowed, while playing at Sardis Road, to manifest, in addition, free-running skills which were otherwise rarely in evidence at the higher level.

During his career he broke numerous records. He was the first player to score more than 1,000 points in Test matches, a feat which he accomplished while bagging 28 points for Wales against France in March 2001, having accumulated that total by scoring in every possible manner, namely a try, four conversions, three penalties and two dropped-goals. When he retired from international rugby in 2003 he held the world points scoring record in Test matches with a total of 1,049 points, which was subsequently bettered by Johnny Wilkinson and Dan Carter. He broke records right up to his last season as a player, for in 2003–4 he kicked a world record 44 consecutive place-kicks with the Celtic Dragons.

With Arwel Thomas and Jonathan Davies, who had now returned to rugby union with the Cardiff club, in contention for the outside-half position in the Wales team, Neil was once again dropped by the Welsh selectors for the autumn international against Australia in 1996 but came on as a replacement full-back. He reluctantly agreed to play in that position for the following game against South Africa, and was selected there on six occasions during the next year or so. However following a 60–26 thrashing by England in February 1998, Neil informed the selectors that he would never play in that position again. Ironically, it was while playing full-back for the 1997 British Lions against the Springboks that he excelled on the world stage.

While his general play was in no way inferior, his remarkable place-kicking was the determining factor in ensuring that the Lions won the series 2–1. During the first Test he kicked five penalties in a 26–16 victory, in the second he again relentlessly converted five penalties in a score line of 18–15 (to the utter desperation of the Springboks whose three kickers failed with numerous attempts at goal). The third Test was convincingly won by the home team, 35–16, with Neil getting nine points for the Lions, giving him a total of 41 points for the series which again was a record. He also made one Test appearance as a Lions replacement on their 2001 tour to Australia, where Johnny Wilkinson was the first-choice fly-half. He returned to South Africa with the Lions in 2009 as a specialist kicking coach and served in a similar capacity on the Lions tour to Australia in 2013. Following his success in 1997 with the British Lions in South Africa, the Grogg shop in Pontypridd, in his honour, made a limited edition Grogg of Neil. Out of the 100 which were produced, three were in British Lions colours, one of which is owned by the player himself, one by his mother while the other was bought by an Ebbw Vale man for £4,100!

There is no doubt that during Graham Henry's tenure as national coach, particularly during his undefeated ten-match run in 1999–2000, Neil's profile as a linking outside-half blossomed. However his kicking prowess, too, was outstanding and during that invincible period he recorded some remarkable personal scoring tallies, for example 19 points against France in March 1999, followed by 30 points against Italy, 22 points against England, 36 points in two games against Argentina, 19 against South Africa, 28 points against Canada, 19 against Japan and in the pre-World Cup fixture against France in August 1999 he equalled the world record when kicking nine penalties in his total of 29 points. This led to Graham Henry declaring that he was the best kicker he had ever worked with, even surpassing Grant Fox, the great All Black outside-half.

However Henry also rated Neil highly for other reasons. He was a great admirer of Neil's distribution skills and of his mastery of the flat pass which his fly-half utilised with such telling effect. It was also a period during which Neil, in the tradition of some notable All Black number tens, revelled in his controlling influence on matches from the outside-half position. To his wily tactical awareness he also added such attributes as solid defensive play and great durability and determination.

Of all his remarkable scoring kicks it is more than likely that the most memorable one for Wales supporters would be his conversion of Scott Gibbs's last-gasp try to snatch victory for Wales against England, and thus deny them of the Grand Slam and Triple Crown, at Wembley in 1999. Neil had already kept his country in the game with six penalty goals and when Gibbs had danced his way through the England defence to touch down the fly-half still needed to kick the conversion for Wales to take the lead. He had been shouting at the centre to try and touch down nearer the posts in order to make the kick a little easier but in the deafening cauldron of sound that was Wembley at that moment his plea went unheard. Gibbs ran back, handed him the ball and said "Just f★★★★★★ kick it!"

By his own admission Neil never got nervous when taking kicks regardless of how crucial they might be. Even at King's Park, Durban when playing for the Lions against South Africa, his kicking drill remained unchanged. He would take deep breaths and imagine he was back at Cae Fardre, a field near his home where he spent hours on end taking practice kicks as a young lad, thus blotting out all noise and removing all pressure. Therefore while there were countless supporters' hearts in countless supporters' mouths before that Wembley conversion, Neil as usual, and with a minimum of fuss, did the business!

Having worked during his early days in his father's scrap yard business he was then employed, until rugby union became a professional sport, by a local firm called Just Rentals. In 2004 he was appointed as a kicking skills coach working with the WRU Academies, following which he joined the national squad in 2006 as a skills coach where he remains today. Always modest, approachable and unassuming he was awarded the MBE in 2000 for services to sport. Directly from that ceremony at Buckingham Palace he was flown by helicopter to play for Cardiff against Saracens – and scored all of his side's points in their 24–14 victory!

BARRY JOHN

THERE IS NO doubt that, had financial remuneration on current scales been available to rugby players during the Barry John era, he would have been a millionaire several times over. Similarly, some would say that if he were playing rugby today Barry John would be a very rich man indeed. However this latter assertion would be completely misleading, for, by his own admission, he would not have been attracted to rugby in its present form but would have turned to another sport, probably soccer. The round ball had always appealed to him and at one point, as a young enthusiast, he was almost snapped up by Coventry City, which was at that time one of the more ambitious clubs in the Football League.

He would claim that in the modern game instinct and flair have been sacrificed at the altar of regimentation and a preoccupation with defensive principles. Players are disinclined to attempt the unorthodox and are too often encumbered by the basic tenet that the best and safest form of attack is to boot the ball as far as possible downfield in the hope of forcing the opponents to yield territorial advantage, tactics which are usually to the detriment of spectators' enjoyment. In addition, he bemoans the fact that the current emphasis on bulk, in addition to creating more spatial limitations on the field of play, deprives many prospective players who are perhaps small in stature from taking up the game. During the amateur days, however, one of the beauties of rugby was that it was a game for all shapes and sizes.

It is not difficult to understand why the unadventurous nature of the game today would be anathema to Barry John. He thrived on a form of rugby which allowed him to provide entertainment while exercising exceptional skills and enthralling spontaneity. He could accomplish feats on the field which no other player was equipped to emulate and which would leave opponents and spectators alike wondering how on earth such play had been at all possible. He appeared to defy the limitations of time and space, often assuming an apparitional aura as he ghosted his way through a seemingly impenetrable defence or through gaps that were visible to nobody else. Many a bewildered opponent left in his wake would often be reminded of a slogan so frequently applied to magicians, "Now you see him now you don't!"

In his day, Barry John was the first superstar of rugby with a standing in the rugby world which compared with the status afforded George Best (with whom Barry became good friends) in football circles. Perhaps an example of the attractions of his talent is the fact that, upon his retirement from rugby in 1972, he was offered £120,000 to play rugby for South California in a new league to be established in the USA. It was a deal, brokered by his good friend, the actor Stanley Baker, which he had to turn down because of other commitments, as indeed was the offer to play American Football as purely a goal-kicker.

His innate talents were boundless. He possessed a devastating sidestep off either foot but could just as effortlessly leave opponents clutching thin air with a subtle sway of the hips, an outrageous dummy or a deceptive dip of the shoulders. The effectiveness of each of these manoeuvres was enhanced by a mesmeric, swaying style of running, with the ball held in both hands before him, while appearing to eye the next obstacle beyond the one with which he was immediately confronted. In addition, a laconic pause whilst engaging his repertoire of ploys, followed by a sudden burst, would also see off numerous would-be tacklers. One of the traits that distinguished him from most other outside-halves was his composure in creating time and space for himself, sometimes when seemingly under pressure, to the extent that he would often appear languid and detached, but nonetheless completely focussed.

To Barry John rugby was essentially about scoring tries and, although his handling and running skills were unsurpassed to that end, he was also a superb kicker of the ball, a skill at which he excelled, both from the hand and when aiming for goal. His round-the-corner style of kicking the dead ball with the instep, a comparatively recent innovation in his era, was particularly successful, at a time when balls were susceptible to absorbing water and became unnaturally heavy, with trajectories that were often unreliable. He was also one of the best exponents in world rugby of the drop-goal. Indeed, by his own admission, one of the highlights of his period with the Cardiff club was, in one game against Llanelli, kicking four drop-goals to defeat his former team by 12–9.

When asked years ago to name the most important aspect of fly-half play he replied that it was the ability to read a game. This was a facet that Barry had mastered during his early years at senior level. He viewed a game as would a chess player regard the pieces before him and, in the manner of the better exponents of that particular board game, would invariably be a few moves ahead of his

© Getty Images

opponents. Coupled with this intuitive aspect of his game was an ability to exploit the opposition's movements to his team's advantage. He believed implicitly in his own ability to get the better of his adversaries as he wished, which, in the light of his laid-back demeanour, sometimes bordered on arrogance. Nonetheless, such an attitude often instilled a similar confidence in his fellow players, which was always to the benefit of team morale.

He was raised in a rugby-loving family in the village of Cefneithin. His eldest brother, Del, captained the village team and siblings Alan and Clive both played for Llanelli. While a pupil at Gwendraeth Grammar School, Barry was immersed in the school's traditional rugby values but despite appearances in regional trials as a scrum-half he failed to win representative honours as a schoolboy. Having converted at the age of 16 to the outside-half position, he played in five matches at first-class level for Llanelli while still at school during the 1963–4 season. It had always been his ambition to wear the scarlet shirt and as a lad spent many hours on the Tanner Bank at Stradey where he would make a point of following every move made by his childhood hero Carwyn James, who also hailed from Cefneithin.

Neither was Barry ever selected for the Welsh Secondary Schools team, much to his disappointment. Were it not for the encouragement of Carwyn he might have turned his back on rugby but he regained his appetite for the game as a student at Trinity College, Carmarthen and with the Llanelli club. He soon became a firm favourite at Stradey and as a result of some sterling performances he won his first two caps for Wales as a Llanelli player. He made his international debut against Australia in December 1966 and won a further 24 caps until his retirement from international rugby in March 1972.

In 1967, at the age of 21, and after four seasons with Llanelli (for whom he scored 199 points in 86 matches, a total which included 25 drop-goals) and despite several enticements to remain at Stradey, Barry decided to join the Cardiff club. His career there spanned five seasons and in 93 matches he scored 363 points, comprising 24 tries and 30 drop-goals. Despite having been disregarded by Wales during 1967 and having had a rather inconsistent Five Nations Championship in 1968, he was selected to tour South Africa with the British Lions later that year. After some impressive performances in provincial matches, he was selected to play against the Springboks in the first Test. Some 15 minutes into the game the Lions were awarded a penalty in their own 25 area, whereupon Barry was told by his captain, Tom Kiernan, to bang the ball into touch. Never one to be constrained by the instructions of a third party, he took a quick tap penalty and sidestepped and shimmied past some four defenders during a 60-yard run only to be literally collared from behind by the renowned South African flanker, Jan Ellis, with the try-line in his sights. Barry fell awkwardly and broke his collar bone, which meant that he never played another game on that tour. When he returned home he turned down an offer of £8,500, in addition to match fees, bonuses and a part-time teaching job, from St Helens to play rugby league. This was the third offer to 'go North' that he had received up until that time.

In 1969 he made a significant contribution to the Wales Five Nations Championship-winning side. During the victory, by 30–9 against England at the Arms Park, in his eleventh game for his country, he scored his first try for Wales, in a manner which left spectators gasping in amazement and which became typical of his precocious talents. Having gathered his own short chip ahead some 30 yards from the visitors' line he went, in his own words, "on a zigzag run checking one way to go past one opponent, sidestepping the other way to get around another, dropping a shoulder next. Done at pace, soon I was over in the corner." John Dawes, playing in the centre, later claimed that he had been fooled three times during that run into thinking that Barry was going to pass to him! The score was described in the press the following day as 'poetry in motion'.

Yet Barry considered his try in Paris in 1971, when Wales beat France by 9–5 (their first win there since 1957) to be his best for his country. The home team had taken the lead through a try by Dauga and the 6' 5" and 15½ stone French number eight was on the point of touching down for another when he was forced into touch by Barry, who suffered a broken nose in the process. Not renowned for his tackling (whilst never one to shirk his tackling duties it wasn't one of his favourite pursuits!) the fly-half later disarmingly shrugged off his heroics by asking who had pushed him into Dauga! Having had his nose painfully reset within minutes on the touchline, he returned to the fray despite being in great discomfort.

In an extremely tight match, with Wales leading 6–5, Barry took the ball, following a Jeff Young heel against the head, some 20 yards from the French line, in what appeared to be a rather confined space. "… I noticed my opposing fly-half Bérot slightly out of position. I stepped nine inches in the other direction and started a sweeping run, gliding down the blindside as a number of French players converged upon me. The nearest was Bertranne, but at the last moment I changed course again, wrong-footed him and swept over for the try." The victory gave Wales their first Grand Slam for 19 years.

Barry's reputation as the best outside-half in the world was firmly established on the British Lions' historic tour to New Zealand in 1971. He appeared in three provincial matches before the first Test in Dunedin and soon aroused the attention of the public and the press. Playing regularly behind a formidable pack, which had not been the case when he played for Wales, he thrived on the quality of possession he received and frequently displayed his range of diverse talents. His mystifying running skills were often in evidence on the tour and were best encapsulated in the try he scored against the New Zealand Universities (a slightly misleading name in that any one who had been to one of the country's universities in the past could represent the team, which meant that there were several All Blacks in the side!).

Receiving the ball from Chico Hopkins, the Lions scrum-half in that particular match, some 20 yards from the opposition line, Barry dummied as if to go for a drop-goal, taking two prospective tacklers out of the game. He then sold another dummy giving the impression that he was going to pass to John Dawes but which was enough to cause a third defender to fall flat on his back, before beating the full-back with a devastating sidestep to cross under the posts. The seemingly impossible score and the apparent ease with which he breached the Universities' defence was, in the first instance, greeted with such deathly silence by the spectators that Barry thought that the referee had blown for an infringement. However, in due course, the whole crowd erupted in applause, the delay being the result of their amazement and incredulity that such a score had been at all possible! The Lions won the game 27–6, with Barry being responsible for 21 of those points.

His reputation as an excellent tactical kicker had been firmly established before he arrived in New Zealand but the tour served to underline his mastery of that particular skill. It was seen at its best in the first Test when he clinically tormented and teased Fergie McCormick, as the experienced All Blacks full-back desperately tried to retrieve Barry's rolling kicks from one corner of the field to the other. That was McCormick's last appearance in an All Black shirt!

The tour was an unprecedented success as the Lions won every provincial game and, for the first time ever in New Zealand, were victors in the Test series by 2–1, with one Test drawn. It was generally agreed that, although a number of players in the Lions party had played exceptionally well, the most influential contributor to their success was Barry John, particularly when capitalising as ever on an excellent service from Gareth Edwards. He appeared in 17 of the 26 games played on the tour (only two players in the party played in more), and scored 191 points, comprising six tries, 31 conversions, eight drop-goals and 27 penalties. This tally included 30 of the 48 points scored by the Lions in the four Tests. His record there as a prolific goal-kicker was more remarkable perhaps in that Barry was only asked to take place-kicks for Wales in his last six appearances for his country, during which he scored 60 points.

It was nevertheless a demanding tour, with the Lions having to face a level of physicality that sometimes bordered on downright thuggery. As a personal protest against such brutality by the Hawke's Bay team in one match, Barry fielded a long kick downfield in his 25, late in the game, and sat on the ball to await the laborious arrival of some fuming opposition forwards, whereupon he picked it up and nonchalantly banged it back upfield to the point from where they had started their vain pursuit. As a result he was criticised by both the British and New Zealand press for his actions, which they considered to be unsporting and arrogant. In Barry's view, however, it was a legitimate way of drawing attention to his disdain for the barbaric tactics employed by the home team.

Conversely there were occasions when he won admiration for his congeniality and unpretentiousness. Having been rested for the game against Manawatu he received a letter from an irate pensioner protesting fiercely against his exclusion and complaining that she had been saving her money for some time especially to see him play. Barry's response was to call unannounced upon the old lady to apologise personally and in no time at all he was the guest of honour at a street party hastily arranged by her neighbours!

As a result of his achievements on the tour he was dubbed 'the King' by his fellow players, a title which was avidly embraced by the media, and on his return home he was indeed given a royal welcome wherever he went. He received countless invitations to receptions, award ceremonies, opening ceremonies, dinners and charity events etc. Sack-loads of letters asking for his autograph would arrive every day, while some autograph hunters would even knock on his door. He worked for Forward Trust, a financial arm of Midland Bank, and people would call at the firm's office expressly to catch a glimpse of Barry John. On one occasion, on a visit to Rhyl to open a new branch of Midland Bank, one of the young girls working there actually curtsied when she was introduced to him. Consequently that particular incident served as a catalyst for his decision to retire from rugby, at the age of 27.

He had initially resumed his rugby career, upon his return from New Zealand, with both Cardiff and Wales. However he found that his celebrity status made such demands upon him that, as well as being totally uncomfortable with the fame that ensued, he felt the standards he set himself as a player were being compromised. As a result he was no longer getting the same pleasure from playing the game. After lengthy discussions with his wife, Jan, and some close friends he announced his retirement in the *Sunday Mirror*, an exclusive for which he received £7,000, in April 1972.

His final appearance on a rugby field was as captain of the Barry John XV against a team assembled by Carwyn James in celebration of the 50th anniversary of the founding of Urdd Gobaith Cymru (the Welsh League of Youth), an occasion on which the cream of British rugby talent was on display. The game's final play comprised a typical piece of Barry John magic, whereby he received the ball some 40 metres from his opponents' line, drifted in and out of the clutches of a number of would-be tacklers, leaving a trail of bamboozled defenders in his wake, to cross for the game's final try. In his desire to finish his career with an act which encapsulated the very essence of the game of rugby in his eyes, namely the scoring of tries, he refused to take the conversion himself, since he did not wish to bring the final curtain down with a kick.

Upon his retirement he maintained his interest in rugby primarily by undertaking a career as a journalist, an occupation which he still pursues. It is certain that during his 40 years in that capacity he has never witnessed the combination of talents that made him, in the opinion of many people, the best outside-half ever. There have been many attempts to define concisely that which made Barry John so special. Norman Mair, the former Scottish international and celebrated rugby writer, famously described him thus: "I was always relieved to see Barry walk through the door to after-match dinners, rather than just materialise through the wall!" Barry's mother, Vimmy, when asked by Chris Lander of the *Mirror* about one of his trademark tries aptly commented, "Well, if Barry had run through a field of daffodils, no one would have noticed". Carwyn James was firmly of the opinion that sporting prowess could sometimes transcend the confines of rules, fitness, coaching and technical excellence to such an extent that, in its pursuit by certain individuals who were inclined to yield to their instinctive nature, it sometimes became an art form. On the rugby field Barry John was the epitome of that theory.

GLYN JOHN

G LYN(DŴR) JOHN HAS a unique place in the history of rugby union in Wales as the only post-war player ever to be allowed back into the 15-a-side fold during the amateur era after playing rugby league as a professional. The case of the brothers Evan and David James, towards the end of the 19th century, served as the only precedent. The Swansea half-backs went to play for Broughton Rangers in Manchester for a signing-on fee of £200 and the sum of £2 per week. As a result they were deemed professionals and were banned for seven years before being reinstated as amateurs by the WRU. Glyn John had signed for Leigh Rugby League Club for the sum of £400 in 1949, playing two matches for them against Hull and York, but soon became disenchanted with the 13-a-side game and sought his reinstatement as an amateur. Since he was just a 17-year-old schoolboy when he joined Leigh his request was granted by the WRU on condition that he returned his signing-on fee.

He was a product of Garw Grammar School and as a talented centre with the school senior XV he represented the Wales Secondary School team. In 1949 he was a member of that team who, in the words of Cliff Morgan, Glyn's outside-half colleague on the day, 'narrowly' defeated England by 30–3 in Cardiff! Playing opposite Glyn in that particular game was Ted Woodward, who was to become a renowned centre for his country and the British Lions. While at school Glyn had shown great aptitude also with the round ball and as a player with Garw Soccer Club played for Wales Youth.

In 1951 he joined Swansea Rugby Club and over a period of two seasons turned out occasionally for the All Whites. He had by that time, however, enrolled at St Luke's College, Exeter, with a view to becoming a school teacher, and appeared regularly for the college team, as well as representing Devon, against impressive opposition. During 1953–4 season, by which time he had also turned out for Aberavon, his exciting, attacking style brought him to the attention of the Wales selectors. He had also joined the RAF and was selected to play for them at rugby. In the first trial for the national side that season he was chosen to play at outside-half opposite Cliff Morgan and in the second trial he played centre alongside Alun Thomas, who had already won a number of caps in that position. He also had an excellent game for the Neath/Aberavon Combined XV against the touring All Blacks.

Since Bleddyn Williams was still suffering from an injury to his leg following the excellent Welsh victory against the All Blacks the previous month, Glyn was selected to play centre in the first Five Nations game against England at Twickenham in 1954, once again alongside Cliff Morgan and Alun Thomas and opposite Ted Woodward. It was, however, rather a disappointing debut for Glyn in a somewhat chaotic match, which England won by 9–6. He missed a few tackles during the game and was called upon to move to outside-half when Rex Willis got injured, since Cliff had to undertake the scrum-half duties. Amusingly, in that capacity Cliff drew the wrath of the front row who claimed he was putting the ball into the scrum on the wrong side!

For the next Wales match against Ireland, although Bleddyn was still unfit, Glyn was demoted to reserve, but was selected as outside-half to play France in the following game when Cliff withdrew through injury. Wales won by 19–13 but it was the last time that Glyn appeared for his country, mainly as a result of pressure from Scotland. They were unable to forget his sojourn with Leigh Rugby League Club and brought persistent protestations to bear on the WRU that in selecting Glyn they were playing someone who was classed as a professional. The WRU capitulated and decided that they would not thereafter select him for the national side.

He continued however to impress in the centre at club level and having joined Cardiff for the 1955–6 season he appeared in 128 games in the next six years. He figured regularly among the Club's leading try scorers and in the game against Watsonians in December 1958 he added four to his tally. During his rugby playing days and after retiring from the game he continued with his career as a schoolmaster at Sedbury Park School, Chepstow and Monmouth School. He sadly died in 1983 at the age of 51.

CLIFF MORGAN

In 1929 CLIFFORD Morgan, at the instigation of his wife, Edith May, decided not to accept an invitation from Tottenham Hotspur to play soccer for them as a professional. Had he not done so Wales might have been deprived of the talents of one of the greatest fly-halves ever, namely his son, called Clifford Isaac Morgan, who one year later was born in the village of Trebanog. In the same way, had he been raised in England, Cliff junior would also have been deprived of the warm, closeted, cultural and chapel-orientated upbringing which the Rhondda Valley could offer at the time. There he was introduced to the activities of such institutions as the Urdd and the eisteddfod which, along with playing the viola in local orchestras and singing in the Port and District Mixed Choir, nurtured his talents as a performer.

Perhaps rather surprisingly Cliff didn't take to playing rugby seriously until he was 16, mainly because Tonyrefail Grammar School had just one team, which catered only for the more senior boys. During his early years, although not immune to the importance of rugby in the local community, soccer was the game which captivated his interest and his ambition was to become a professional footballer. But gradually at the grammar school, due to the influence of Ned Gribble, the master who was in charge of games, rugby became Cliff's passion and under his teacher's tutelage he began to display the skills which would in due course distinguish him as one of the most talented outside-halves in world rugby.

He first won recognition by being selected to play for the Welsh Secondary Schools team on two occasions and was then invited, when still at school, to play for Cardiff in an evening friendly match. In the autumn of 1949 he enrolled at UCW Cardiff to study for a degree in science and also joined the Cardiff club as one of five fly-halves. In that first year he was frequently selected for the club's second team and even played a handful of games for the first XV, alongside such established stars as Haydn Tanner, Jack Matthews and Bleddyn Williams, from whom he received invaluable advice.

By the following year Cliff, who had chosen to forfeit his place at university by declining the offer to resit some of his first-year exams, appeared fairly often for the Cardiff first team. One of the main reasons for his promotion was that the team's regular fly-half, Billy Cleaver, had been selected for the 1950 British Lions and was consequently unavailable for his home club for a period of six months. In due course, over a period of eight years, Cliff appeared in 202 games for Cardiff. He scored 38 tries and made many, many more. During that period he established himself as one of the most exciting and entertaining players in Welsh rugby and as one of the of the original 'Chapel' outside-halves.

His earnest, jinking and thrusting endeavours, when attacking with ball in hand, constantly gave the impression that he was about to burst at the seams as he strove to breach opposing defences. He had a particular knack for spotting an opening and was assisted in his efforts to exploit such a situation by a chunky, strong physique (he was 5' 7" and weighed 12 stone) which, coupled with short bandy legs pumping furiously and a low centre of gravity,

© Getty Images

often enabled him to bounce off imposing defenders. With a liking for taking his scrum-half's pass at speed he would frequently succeed in rounding his markers with a devastating burst of acceleration that would leave them clutching thin air. Alternatively, he could draw on numerous other attributes to achieve the same goal such as a shimmy, to leave would-be tacklers flat-footed, or a devastating sidestep (a skill which he once claimed was developed on a local field in an effort to avoid cowpats when he briefly played for a local team!).

Cliff's success was all the more remarkable in light of the latitude which flankers in particular were allowed by the laws of the game at that time. Since they were permitted to break early from the scrum and line-out, they were often within eye-balling distance of the opposing fly-half before he had received the ball from his scrum-half. In the dramatic words of Clem Thomas, the Swansea and Wales open side wing-forward at the time, "Cliff Morgan played in an era when flankers like myself had a licence to kill outside-halves!"

Despite his reputation as an elusive runner with the ball, Cliff could never be called a selfish player and the phenomenal number of tries scored by three-quarters such as Bleddyn Williams, for club and country, while playing outside him is ample testimony to this fact. For he had one basic philosophy in that respect, namely "everyone knows *when* to do things but only the clever fly-half knows *when not* to do things". In that connection, when the situation so demanded, Cliff was an excellent distributor of the ball and perhaps, despite the teachings of Ned Gribble, a very effective kicker in attack and in defence. For during his schooldays he would be constantly reminded by 'Mr Gribble' that rugby was a handling game. Indeed, on one occasion Cliff was left out of the school team for two weeks by his games master because he had chosen to drop a goal to ensure a narrow victory against Maesteg School when there were players outside him who were in a good position to score a try!

His talents were recognised by the Welsh selectors

when he was chosen, while still only 20 years old, to play against Ireland in Cardiff in 1951. Cliff recalls with great amusement some of the events connected to that occasion and which are testimony to the incredible differences between the treatment of international players today and the way that members of the Welsh team were regarded by the Union at that time. For example, the letter (which was "like a piece of paper you'd whip off a lavatory roll") written by the secretary of the WRU informing Cliff of his selection included the following paragraph:

"You are to wear the white-topped stockings you wore against Scotland [that particular game against Ireland was Cliff's first appearance for Wales!]. Please do not forget to bring them as stockings have become very scarce. Are you going to wear your own white shorts, or do you wish to borrow a pair of the Union's?"

Until he retired in 1958, Cliff was an automatic selection for all but one of the next 29 matches played by Wales (he had been unavailable for three games due to injury). He gave many notable performances during his tenure, such as the game against Ireland in 1952 when Wales clinched another Triple Crown, and was skipper for the 1956 season when Wales won the Five Nations Championship. There were some rare off-days, such as the narrow defeat, by 6–3, against the 1951 Springboks in very heavy conditions, with Cliff, in later years claiming that "my scatter-brained and scattily directed kicking cost Wales the game". However, four years later he was feted by rugby followers and critics throughout South Africa for his memorable performances with the British Lions during their tour there.

It was generally agreed at that time that Cliff was the

finest outside-half who had ever visited South Africa. He played in eleven provincial matches and in the four Tests, having been honoured with the captaincy for the third Test. Despite the undisputed success of the Lions in drawing the series 2–2 it is generally agreed that the highlight of the tour was the brilliant try scored by Cliff in the 23–22 victory in the first Test, in front of over 90,000 spectators. It was a piece of classic Morgan artistry, namely a burst of speed, a shimmy and a swerve around the despairing van Wyk and a touch-down under the posts. For the remainder of the tour Cliff was dubbed 'Morgan the Magnificent' by the national press. The tour was also an unqualified success on a social level, due in no small part to Cliff's charismatic qualities off the field and to his musical talents which were given prominence by his role as the party's choirmaster and pianist. He retired from rugby at the age of 28, playing his last game in Nairobi for the Barbarians, a team he represented on 17 occasions, against East Africa.

He played the occasional game for fun well after that African farewell. Clive Rowlands recalls the time he partnered Cliff, who was a great friend, in a game to celebrate the official opening of the Cwmtwrch Rugby Club clubhouse in 1970. In a memorable speech afterwards he thanked Clive for his magnificent service during the match, but regretted not having sparkled as he would have liked because, having borrowed Clive's boots for the game, every time he wanted to run his boots decided to kick!

Cliff enjoyed enormous success in his career outside rugby. Upon leaving university he first obtained employment as a trainee manager with the Electricity

Board, a post which was not entirely to his liking. After some four years he left to work as manager of a wire-rope factory in Wicklow, during which time he played for one season with the Irish club, Bective Rangers. This was followed by a period of employment as a salesman with a company making laboratory equipment for educational and scientific establishments. During this time Cliff's rugby accomplishments meant that he was very much in demand by the media and his knowledgeable, infectious and ebullient personality led to his being offered a position as sports organiser by BBC Wales.

This, for him, was the beginning of a glittering career in broadcasting, both in production and as a presenter. He progressed to become Editor of *Grandstand*, the top sports programme of the day, head of BBC Radio Outside Broadcasts and then to head of BBC Sport and Outside Broadcasts, a position he held for twelve years. He also spent a period at ITV as editor of the prestigious current affairs programme *This Week*. As a broadcaster he was a popular team captain in the first ever series of a *Question of Sport* and on his retirement from BBC TV in 1987 he made a niche for himself as the presenter of many memorable radio series, such as *Sport on Four*. What is remarkable is that much of his success in broadcasting was achieved despite suffering a serious stroke at the age 41. His first broadcast following his recovery from that illness was the never-to-be-forgotten commentary on Gareth Edwards's wonder try for the Barbarians against the All Blacks in 1973.

Cruelly, the warm, mellow and comforting voice which formed such a great part of his appeal as a radio presenter had been silenced for some time. Due to the ravages of cancer Cliff's larynx had to be removed, which meant that he breathed through his neck and spoke through a small plastic valve. For many years he had enjoyed life with his second wife Pat (his first wife Nuala, after 45 years of marriage, died in 1999) on the Isle of Wight, but sadly passed away in August 2013 after a long illness. Countless friends and admirers paid tribute to a magnificent rugby player and a warm, generous and charismatic human being. Cliff claimed that due to his comparatively small physical stature he would never have been able to play in the modern period against players who are so big, fit and strong. Those who witnessed the talents of Cliff Morgan would disagree entirely, since he possessed exceptional gifts which would see him stand out in any rugby era.

PETER MORGAN

I N HIS SIX games for Wales (two of which were uncapped) Peter played in four different positions, which was evidence of the fact that one of his greatest attributes was his versatility and his ability to apply his diverse skills to meet the varied demands of different aspects of back play. Indeed in 1980, he was describes by a local south Wales newspaper as 'a jack of most out-of-scrum trades'. He was first asked to don the Wales jersey as full-back in an uncapped match against Romania at Cardiff Arms Park in October 1979. His selection surprised many critics in that, despite his commendable form for the Scarlets at outside-half, which was his favoured position, or sometimes in the centre, he had previously played in the full-back position on just three occasions. Nevertheless, he gave an exceptional performance on the day as Wales struggled to defeat the visitors by 13–12.

He was generally acclaimed to be a 'natural footballer' and although such a description could validly be applied to most international outside-halves, it was not always a pertinent pre-conception when assessing the attributes of players in that position. To merit the accolade 'footballer', the subject would have to be an excellent handler and distributor of the ball, a deceptive and imaginative runner, an accomplished kicker, an acute observer of play around him and someone who exuded an air of having matters under control. All of these talents were manifested in Peter's play from a very young age and during 1979, at the age of 20 years old, he was chosen as Wales' Most Promising Player by the Welsh Rugby Writers Association. His rise to prominence, mainly as an able deputy for Phil Bennett at Stradey, had been remarkably sudden.

He was born in Broadhaven and honed his rugby skills as a young lad on the local beach. Following his education at Sir Thomas Picton Secondary School, Haverfordwest, where he benefited greatly from the tutelage of his PE teacher, Peter Herbert, he began playing for Haverfordwest Rugby Club Youth XV and won two caps for his country at that level. Having joined the Scarlets soon after, he profited greatly from the coaching of Carwyn James and the opportunity of playing with Phil Bennett. In September 1978 he represented the Scarlets for the first time against Pontypridd and at the end of that season he gained great experience from going on tour with Llanelli to South Africa.

He won his first of four caps against Scotland, at the Arms Park, on 1 March 1980, when he played in the centre position as a replacement for the injured outside-half, Gareth Davies (with David Richards moving from centre to take up the number ten role), which he later described "as a terrifying experience"! Wales were victorious by 17–6 and Peter was selected to play in the next match against Ireland at outside-half, since Gareth Davies was still injured. It was considered by the selectors that David Richards should continue as centre since Peter's tactical kicking in support of his pack, a commodity for which Gareth Davies was renowned, was superior. Wales unfortunately were well beaten by 21–7, as Ireland crossed for three tries, their highest number against Wales since 1932.

The next Wales game was in September 1980 when an uncapped match was held against an Overseas XV as part of the WRU centenary celebrations. On that occasion Peter came on as a replacement for Pat Daniels on the left wing! Wales were the victors by 32–25 in a match which perhaps offered two lasting memories. Firstly, the Swansea full-back Roger Blythe scored three tries in his personal total of 24 points. The game also saw the deployment of the 'flying wedge', by the Overseas XV, a tactic introduced by their coach, Stan Addicott (who also acted in that capacity with Swansea Rugby Club) to score one of their tries. This was a move that was eventually banned by the rugby authorities. Two months later Peter appeared as a replacement for Wales against New Zealand in Cardiff, this time on the right wing, when the home team was comprehensively beaten.

Although recent performances by the Wales team had been disappointing, Peter's varied talents had been noted, in particular his ability to play in a number of positions with a marked degree of flair. As a result, although comparatively inexperienced at international level, he was chosen to tour South Africa with the British Lions in the summer of 1980 as an utility back. He was the youngest in the party and probably the most surprising selection. However his versatility was deployed to good advantage from the beginning of the tour since in the first four matches in which he participated he once again played in four different positions. The Lions, of course, despite losing the Test series 3–1, won all their provincial games. Peter played in seven of these, but without once being selected as outside-half. He reserved his best performance until the final provincial match against Griqualand West, when he scored a try and a dropped-goal in a Lions victory by 23–19. According to John Reason, the respected *Daily Telegraph* rugby correspondent, they "thus preserved their [provincial] unbeaten record, which extended back to 1966, and they were delighted about the contribution that Peter Morgan made to that victory".

He made just one more appearance for his country when he was selected as centre against Ireland in Cardiff in February 1981, a match for which long-serving members of the team, J.P.R. Williams, Steve Fenwick and Gareth Davies were sensationally dropped. It was however a game which Peter would rather forget for he was forced to leave the field having suffered three broken ribs when taking a 'hospital' pass from outside-half, Gary Pearce!

He retired from first-class rugby in 1988 having given ten years of excellent service to the Llanelli club, during which he made over 300 appearances. The varied skills that he had displayed throughout his career were of course ideally suited to seven-a-side rugby, a game at which he excelled, and as a member of the victorious Llanelli team in the Snelling Sevens Competition of 1979 he was awarded the Bill Everson Trophy as the Outstanding Player of the Tournament. A coal-merchant and builder by trade, he later turned his attention to local government and was elected chairman of Pembrokeshire County Council for 2012–13. He unfortunately suffered a stroke during the summer of 2012 but returned in due course to resume his duties as chairman.

GARY PEARCE

B ORN IN LAUGHARNE in 1960 he played for the Welsh Secondary Schools team and won Welsh Youth caps, at outside-half and centre, with both the Laugharne and Carmarthen Athletic Clubs. Having initially been attracted to Stradey, he moved to Bridgend in 1979 where he remained until he rejoined the Scarlets in 1983. Indeed, having toured with Wales to North America as a 19 year old in 1980, he was the leading scorer in Welsh rugby in 1981–2, with 391 points for Bridgend. He won his three Welsh caps while playing at the Brewery Field, alongside his club partner, Gerald Williams. The first was against Ireland at the Arms Park in February 1981 when he was selected instead of Gareth Davies who, along with J.P.R. Williams and Steve Fenwick, had been dropped following the Wales defeat at Murrayfield.

In that game Gary made a notable contribution to the Wales victory by 9–8, in that it was his drop-goal, via his weaker left foot, ten minutes from the end that sealed the win. He had initially started running with the ball but saw that the Irish centres were rapidly converging upon him which led him, fortunately, to check and deliver the crucial kick. Indeed, on the day, his running game had proved to be effective, yet he himself was disappointed with his kicking. He admitted to losing concentration for some 20 minutes when one of his clearance kicks was charged down which resulted in an Irish try. He had also been responsible for delivering a hospital pass to Peter

Morgan which caused the centre to leave the field with three broken ribs! In an effort to secure touch more often, Gary shortened his line kicking which led some critics to lament the loss of the prodigious length obtained by Gareth Davies in that respect.

Gary retained his place for the next game against France which Wales narrowly lost by 19–15 in which he played an important part in a memorable score by centre, David Richards. Upon the return of Gareth Davies for the start of the following season's Five Nations Championship Gary was on the replacements bench against Ireland in Dublin. However, he took the field when the Cardiff player got injured, and kicked a drop-goal, which unfortunately did not serve to save Wales from defeat by 20–12. He was never to wear the Wales jersey again but played superbly for Bridgend for the remainder of the season. His ability to carve openings and to burst through opposing defences with a deceptive turn of speed, notwithstanding his stocky appearance, delighted his followers. He was also a sound and reliable kicker from the hand as well as being a prolific place-kicker.

Following his return to Llanelli in 1983 he continued to excel. He made a significant contribution to the Scarlets victory over the touring Wallabies in 1984 but his supreme achievement in Llanelli colours is generally recognised to be his last-ditch drop-goal to win the 1985 Schweppes Cup final at the Arms Park. With little remaining of the time added on for injuries, Cardiff, the clear favourites to win the trophy, were ahead by 14–12. Remarkably, from a line-out just inside their opponents' 22-metre line, the Llanelli pack gained possession and fed their half-backs. Gary received the ball some ten metres in from the left-side touchline and struck probably his sweetest drop-goal ever, to win the game. The following season he continued in his productive vein and broke the Club record by amassing 420 points. When he left Stradey in 1986 to play rugby league with Hull he had represented the Scarlets 136 times, scoring 32 tries and kicking 161 penalties.

His introduction to the 13-a-side game was rather tough and it took him some two years to establish himself in the North. However, in due course he became a much respected League outside-half, firstly with Hull, for whom, until his departure in 1990, he scored 649 points, including 23 tries. He then joined Sheffield, Scarborough Pirates and finally Ryedale York. While with the latter two clubs he gained four rugby league caps for Wales. His chunky and sturdy build, coupled with effective mobility also allowed him to play as a hooker towards the close of his League career.

When that came to an end he agreed to help out as player-coach for the short term with Pocklington Rugby Union Club. He remained there for eight years leading the club to numerous honours, namely winning three championship titles and being voted in 1999–2000 as the *Rugby World* magazine British Team of the Year. From 2000–5 he was player-director of rugby with Hull Rugby Union Club, leading them to two promotions in three seasons. He is currently the head coach at Hull Ionians Rugby Union Club who gained promotion last season to the English National League Division One, which Gary described as one of the proudest achievements in his rugby career.

ALAN REES

DESPITE THE FACT that he played first-class rugby to the highest level and was awarded three caps for his country, Alan Rees was probably more renowned in Wales as a cricketer with Glamorgan. He made his first-class debut as a 17 year old against Somerset at Weston-super-Mare in 1955 and eventually made 216 appearances for the county. He won his county cap in 1963 and his talents as a mid-order batsman (he scored a total of 7,618 runs) and medium-pace bowler were greatly appreciated. However his main attribute was the excellence of his fielding in the covers and, during his prime, he was recognised as one of the best in the world in that position.

In that respect his talent was recognised by the England selectors in 1964 when they summoned him to act as a substitute fielder in the third Ashes Test against Australia, during which he made his mark by catching Peter Burge off the bowling of Freddie Trueman. During that year he was also a member of the Glamorgan side that famously defeated the Australians, a feat which he and the team repeated in 1968. He somewhat infamously made the headlines again the following year when during a match against Middlesex at Lords, he was given out for 'handling the ball' which was only the second time ever that such a decision had been given in the County Championship.

He first came to prominence as a rugby player at Glan Afan Grammar School, Port Talbot from where he was selected to represent the Welsh Secondary Schools team.

His first two appearances in 1954 and 1955 were at centre, before he reverted to his favoured outside-half position for his remaining Secondary Schools appearances. In 1956 he was chosen to tour South Africa with the Young Dragons in celebration of the 50th anniversary of the formation of the Welsh Secondary Schools Association. The tour was a remarkable success, with the team losing just one game, drawing another and securing six victories against notable provincial opposition, such as the formidable Transvaal team, at Ellis Park. Having excelled in the earlier part of that match Alan then got injured, with the result that he was unable to play in the final three games. However, he had already established himself as an extremely gifted outside-half who won the admiration of many rugby followers in the country. After his third game a local reporter wrote, 'Rees showed why he is regarded as the logical successor to Cliff Morgan' and of the eight tries scored by the Dragons in that match seven were attributed to the skilful contribution of Alan Rees.

During that tour he had the opportunity to play outside Clive Rowlands who, on their return home, became a good friend when they were both posted to the same barracks when undertaking National Service. Although officially a radar mechanic, Alan played rugby twice a week for the RAF against some of the leading sides in England and Wales. He also made appearances for Maesteg, Aberavon and Llanelli, where he teamed up with Onllwyn Brace. However, since other young promising players such as D.K. Jones and Brian Davies were competing for the outside-half position there, he decided to return to Maesteg, whom he captained in 1961–2.

His ability to make telling, electrifying breaks, along

with his accomplished kicking brought him in due course to the attention of the Welsh selectors. In the autumn of 1961 he was selected for the Probables team in the final Welsh trial, in direct opposition to Cliff Ashton, who had already won six caps. Alan had an excellent game scoring two tries in the 20–3 victory and was described in the rugby press following the game as 'the new master' and 'the find of the season'. He was also reported as possessing a cool, big-match temperament and the 'accuracy and balance of an outstanding cricket fielder'.

As a result he was selected for the first game of the Five Nations Championship in 1962 against England at Twickenham which, in the opinion of most critics, would be a baptism of fire for the Maesteg fly-half. For his opposite number was Richard Sharpe who two years previously had ripped the Wales defence apart. However, it was generally agreed that he played well in a fairly drab 0–0 draw, despite the fact that he was often hampered by a slow delivery from the Welsh forwards and the close attention of the England open-side, Budge Rogers. As a result he was often forced to turn inside, away from his centres, and kick, which he did wisely and accurately despite the swirling wind (a factor which was instrumental in Kel Coslett missing five penalty attempts for Wales). On the day Alan also made a couple of testing breaks which showed great promise.

He naturally retained his place for the next game against Scotland at the Arms Park, in atrocious conditions, which the visitors won by 8–3, and for the first time in Cardiff for 40 years. It was a day for kicking, yet Alan was judged to have displayed his inexperience in that respect in that he often kicked too far in front of his forwards to enable them to get under the ball. He did, however, score his country's only points with a drop-goal in the closing stages of the match. His kicking in support of his pack in the game against France seven weeks later was much more disciplined and effective, for he had soon realised that his team's chance of winning (which they did, by 3–0) would be greatly increased if they played with a minimum of risk.

It is said that at the end of that international season he was approached concerning his availability to tour with the British Lions in South Africa that summer but discounted the possibility since he did not wish to miss the forthcoming cricket season, a decision which he subsequently regretted. However rugby enthusiasts in Wales were denied further opportunities to witness his talents since he chose to sign for Leeds Rugby League Club later that year. He had an arrangement with the club whereby he would play rugby league from September until April and then be allowed to return to play for Glamorgan at the start of the cricket season.

He remained with Leeds for three years but was forced to retire because of a knee injury he received in a match against Featherstone Rovers, which plagued him for years afterwards. On his return to Wales he continued with his cricket career until he retired from the first-class Championship game in 1968, but continued to appear in Gillette Cup matches in 1970 and 1971 and in the Sunday League in 1972. He also occasionally turned out, on the right wing, for the Afan Lido soccer team in the Welsh League, played badminton to county level and represented Wales Veterans at squash. After his retirement as a professional cricketer he became deputy sports officer for Afan Borough Council.

BRYAN RICHARDS

BRYAN RICHARDS COULD well have become a first-class cricketer but chose instead to concentrate on rugby. He captained the Welsh Schools cricket team against England at St Helen's, Swansea and played for Glamorgan at Minor Counties level. Yet it was as an accomplished player with Swansea Rugby Club at that St Helen's ground that he made a name for himself. A native of Skewen he began his first-class rugby career with Neath while still a pupil at Neath Grammar School. From there he went to UCW Swansea to study economics and captained the rugby team, while also turning out for Neath when college duties permitted. As a schoolboy he played scrum-half but later developed a preference for the fly-half position, although the debate as to which was his better position continued at the Gnoll. Consequently he left to join the All Whites for the 1954–5 season.

During his second game for the club against Coventry he had the misfortune to break an ankle and a wrist which meant that he was sidelined for the remainder of the season. However, over the next six seasons he played outside-half in 156 matches for Swansea, serving as captain in 1958–9 and delighting the home supporters with his talents. Standing just 5' 8" tall he was a dapper little player who, possessing a natural exuberance for the running game, constantly probed opposing defences with darting, rapier-like breaks. Conversely, although contrary to his naturally enterprising instincts, he was an astute tactical kicker who, when the occasion so demanded, was able to effectively close the game down.

Following his graduation from UCW Swansea Bryan went up to Cambridge to study for a diploma in education, and gained a rugby Blue in 1955. He also represented a Combined Oxford and Cambridge Universities XV on a tour of Argentina. He then did his National Service with the RAF whom he represented at rugby, while also playing for Swansea. During the next few years he frequently appeared in trials for the Wales team but since Cliff Morgan was the first-choice outside-half for his country during most of that period Bryan was hardly in contention for that position in the national team.

However, two years after Cliff's retirement from international rugby, Bryan was selected at long last to play for Wales against France in Cardiff, on 26 March 1960 at the age of 28. The 1959–60 season had been particularly fruitful for him at St Helen's and he had also excelled in the second Welsh trial. In addition, his cause had been helped by the fact that the incumbent Wales fly-half, Cliff Ashton, had played poorly in the previous match against Ireland, in which Wales, despite their victory by one point, had been generally outplayed. However Bryan's debut was a disappointment, as he suffered from the fact that his pack was completely dominated by the French eight, as the visitors romped to victory while scoring four tries to one. Consequently he was tense and nervous throughout and had little opportunity to display the qualities that had made him such a successful fly-half with the All Whites.

He never played for Wales again but continued to shine on the club scene. He had in recent years been employed as a teacher at Christ College, Brecon, but at the end of the 1960–1 season he took a post in the London area and joined London Welsh Rugby Club. For three seasons there he played with his accustomed skill and enterprise and was elected captain in 1963. During his time at Old Deer Park he was also selected to represent the Barbarians and Hampshire. He returned to play for Swansea on one occasion during the 1964–5 season and had two further games during the following season, making his final appearance against Newport in 1966 at the age of 34.

He became, in due course, head of economics at Dulwich College, from where in 1970 he was appointed to the staff of Rugby School. He retired in 1994 as senior housemaster but an achievement which was a great source of pride for him was that at Rugby he had coached, at various times, every one of the school's rugby teams, 16 in all, from the Under 14s to the First XV. By the age of 69 Bryan was blind in one eye as a result of glaucoma and then suffered from macular degeneration which led to him losing his sight in the other eye. That particular condition was alleviated through laser treatment in 2002 and, despite the fact that he was left with a little blurred, peripheral vision, he was registered as blind.

However that did not entail that Bryan was happy to be confined to inactivity. He was soon introduced to the English Blind Golfing Association (one of whose many patrons, ironically, was Cliff Morgan). Playing off a handicap of 28, with a sighted golfer to guide him around the course, Bryan, following an intense selection process over a number of days, was chosen to play for England against Scotland. He was naturally subjected to a great deal of banter from friends that he deigned to represent the red rose but was able to justify his decision by virtue of the fact that Wales did not have a Blind Golf team! In due course he became captain and then secretary of the Association and in the latter post was able to use his influence to get the name of his native country recognised in its title, with the result that it is now officially known as the England and Wales Blind Golfing Association. He is still playing golf at the age of 81 and, although not a current member of the England team, he is ranked 13th in the Association's Order of Merit for 2012–13.

KEN RICHARDS

L IKE ALAN REES, who succeeded him as outside-half in the Wales team, Ken Richards went to rugby league when in his prime, following just one season on the international stage. However, he was introduced to that stage at the comparatively mature age of 26 years old. As a member of the Bridgend Grammar School team he was selected for the Welsh Secondary Schools team. Then, having appeared for Tondu and Maesteg, he spent two years with Swansea between 1952–4. His first season saw him play in 30 matches but during the following year he made just 13 appearances, with the result that he sought pastures new at the Arms Park.

The Cardiff club were looking for an outside-half to fill the void left by Cliff Morgan's departure to play for Bective Rangers and Ken was one of a number of candidates hoping to become established in that position. In 1954–5, his first season at the Arms Park, he was awarded his club cap and the fact that he played 37 games for the Black and Blues in his second season, during which he scored 121 points, including nine tries, would suggest that he was by then the preferred choice. However, his appearances for the next few seasons were sporadic with the result that, having played in the first team on only four occasions in the 1959–60 season, during the opening months, he decided to leave the Cardiff club. In six seasons there he made 112 appearances, scoring 218 points, a total which included 30 tries.

In 1960 he joined Bridgend, his hometown club, and soon delighted their supporters with his exhilarating play, scoring some of the most exciting individual tries that they had ever witnessed. His long-legged physique, which gave being to a deceptively loping stride and a telling sidestep enabled him to breach the most resolute defence. He was also an excellent controller of proceedings on the pitch, a facet which was complemented by his invaluable talents as a kicker, both tactically and as a points scorer. He was renowned as a drop-goal specialist who would frequently resort to that method when kicking conversions and penalty goals. At the end of 1960–1 he was the top scorer in Welsh rugby with 289 points.

Despite having been ignored by the Welsh selectors for inclusion in the pre-international trial teams, Ken Richards won five caps in 1960–1, the first of which was against the Springboks in December 1960 at the Arms Park. He had displaced Bryan Richards in the fly-half position (who had a disappointing debut for Wales against France in the previous game) but on the day Ken couldn't have imagined being asked to make his debut in more atrocious playing conditions. The pitch was a sea of mud, the rain poured down and an icy, debilitating wind made it impossible for him, or any other back, to make any kind of impression. So much so that the referee asked Terry Davies, the Wales captain, 15 minutes from the end, whether the Wales team wished to carry on playing! In a forward-dominated match South Africa won by one penalty goal to nil, although Ken came close to snatching a draw for Wales with an attempted drop-goal. He did, however, earn one particular distinction during the game – he became the first Wales outside-half to wear number ten on his back. Previously players in that position had worn the number six jersey.

In his next match for Wales, against England at the Arms Park, Ken orchestrated his three-quarter line to play effective running rugby as Wales earned a magnificent victory by two tries to one (6–3), both scored as a result of thrilling contributions by Dewi Bebb on the left wing. Ken also made three very effective half-breaks but there were some who criticised him for standing too deep behind the scrum, which resulted in his reluctance to bring his three-quarters into play more frequently. However, in the second half he controlled the game admirably, and kicked magnificently in support of his forwards. For, after 47 minutes Wales were reduced to 14 men following the departure of Cyril Davies with a knee injury, whereupon flanker Haydn Morgan had to take up the centre position for the remainder of the game.

Ken, naturally perhaps, kept his place for the next game against Scotland at Murrayfield which turned out to be a dour encounter as Wales lost by three points to nil. In the match against Ireland at Cardiff he cemented his reputation as an international fly-half by obtaining all of his country's points in their 9–0 victory. According to one observer "the game was dominated by the gangly Ken Richards" as he scored an excellent individual try and kicked two penalty goals. However, despite the pleasant conditions, both teams were condemned for their negative tactics with the half-backs on each side, namely Onllwyn Brace and Ken for the home team, being guilty of kicking possession away on numerous occasions. Allied to the fact that, in the words of rugby historians David Smith and Gareth Williams, the exciting talents of the Welsh pair were 'frustrated to impotence as both back lines lay up on each other flatter than last week's beer', the game made for a disappointing spectacle.

Ken's last appearance in the red jersey was in the narrow defeat by 8–6 against France in Paris. Within a few months he had left Wales to join Salford Rugby League Club, but over a period of three seasons he failed to make an impression on that particular game. He made an auspicious start for his new club in September 1961 when he kicked a penalty goal from 50 metres against Doncaster. However, on the whole he had difficulty in adapting to rugby league's defensive systems with the result that his record as a player in that particular code was rather nondescript. Conversely his talents as a Union player on the club scene, as well as on the short-lived international level, were undisputed. He also played with distinction for Glamorgan and the RAF.

In 1964 he returned to his native Bridgend and resumed his career as a schoolteacher, at Heol Gam Secondary School. In January 1972, at the age of 37 years old, he was tragically killed in a road accident.

MARK RING

Mark Ring played 32 times for Wales over a period of nine years, with 27 appearances in the centre, one at full-back and four at outside-half. It is possible, had he been fully fit throughout that period, that the total number of international caps would have been considerably greater, but two serious injuries in particular prevented him from playing for lengthy periods. Such absences deprived Wales of the talents of an exciting and adventurous player who, in the opinion of many critics and peers, was one of the most naturally gifted performers of his era. However his sometimes ill-disciplined and seemingly carefree approach brought criticism from many detractors. Although his creativity and flair would often bring their rewards his unpredictability, as he sought to surprise the opposition with the unexpected, would sometimes confuse his own players, to the detriment of the team. Even so, such was his confidence in his own ability that even the occasional debacle would do nothing to diminish his enthusiasm.

Perhaps an example of his misplaced inventiveness was the occasion, during a game against London Welsh in 1989, when he chose to back-heel a conversion and hit the crossbar. He claimed, having failed with three previous orthodox attempts and having had to suffer the consequent abuse of a heckler in the crowd, that he thought it would be a good idea to try something different! As a result he was forced by the Cardiff committee to write a letter of apology to London Welsh and banned from taking club place-kicks for two years.

He started to excel at rugby at primary school in Cardiff, gaining his first representative honour of note in a game between East Wales and West Wales Under 12s in 1974 at the Arms Park, when he was in direct opposition to another young starlet, Jonathan Davies. He progressed through the junior ranks of Cardiff Rugby Club and having captained the Cardiff Youth team, in what was to be an unbeaten season, he was selected for the Wales Youth team. He made his senior debut for Black and Blues at the age of 18, and soon gained selection for the Wales B team. However, whereas he had played most of his rugby, prior to reaching senior level, as a fly-half, the Cardiff club preferred to play him in the centre. After just twelve games in that position he was selected, at the age of 20, for Wales against England at Cardiff in February 1983, as a replacement for the injured Robert Ackerman. In June 1984 he won his first cap for his country at baseball, the fourth Wales rugby player to achieve this feat (another was his contemporary, David Bishop).

He did not play rugby again for Wales until November 1984, when he was selected to face Australia having been a member of the Cardiff team that beat the tourists in October. Against Wales however Australia were convincing winners but Ring kept his place against Scotland, Ireland and France in the following Five Nations Championship matches. Indeed, up until that point, despite the fact that Wales had lost all four fixtures that season, 'Ringo' had established himself as an accomplished centre who had an adventurous, precocious approach to his game. His vision and penetrative running led to his making a number of exciting breaks and his overall form led to his being voted Welsh Player of the Year by the *Western Mail*. In the light of his exuberant club performances he was also chosen as Cardiff Player of the Year by supporters. However, in April 1985, he was cruelly struck down by a bad knee injury sustained in a tackle during a club match against Swansea.

After being out of rugby for almost a year he regained his place in the Wales team for the game against Ireland in April 1987 and played in ten international matches, including the 1987 World Cup in New Zealand, until June 1988, when he appeared at full-back on the Wales tour to New Zealand. By that time he had decided to leave Cardiff for Pontypool Rugby Club, mainly because he had been offered an opportunity to play in his favoured fly-half position, alongside his friend David Bishop. The 1987–8 season with the Gwent team was probably his most successful period ever as a club player and coincided with perhaps the most productive season in the club's history, during which they were without doubt the best side in Wales, if not Great Britain. Between 1983–6 Ray Prosser had guided the club to three Welsh Championships, a feat repeated under Bobby Windsor's tenure as coach and Mark Ring's inspirational play during that 1987–8 season.

Mark was initially unsure as to the kind of welcome he would receive at Pontypool Park, particularly when Ray Prosser, who was still on the committee, came up to him during his first training session with his new club and said, "What are you doin' 'ere son, this is a Valleys club?!" However, he soon became a great favourite and during the season scored 357 points from 32 games, comprising 14 tries, 59 conversions, 47 penalties and 14 drop-goals, as the team won 40 of its 42 matches. He was made to realise the significance of his contribution when Ray Prosser, who considered three-quarters to be 'prima donnas', described Bishop and Mark Ring as the best half-back pairing in the world! However he left Pontypool after one season and rejoined Cardiff.

He continued to play for Wales in the centre, with the exception of that second Test in New Zealand in June 1988. Although he was a member of the squad to face Romania in December 1988, he was later dropped for missing training. He claimed that confusion between dates for national duties and commitments with the Barbarians had been responsible for his non-appearance at the squad session. However he later admitted that during that particular week he was required by Wigan Rugby League Club to come to a decision as to whether he wished to sign for them, which had contributed to his confusion regarding his squad duties.

Wigan had offered him £95,000 over four seasons, with £50,000 to be paid immediately. He would also receive a weekly wage plus a £270 bonus for every win with the first team and a £130 win bonus when playing for the reserves. The club had previously made Ringo an offer which was not quite so lucrative but for the second time he decided to remain a union player, although admitting that, as a young civil servant taking home less than £100 pounds a week, he had been tempted. Shortly after being disciplined before the Romania game he was again badly injured in a club match which entailed his missing the whole of the 1989 Five Nations campaign and being bypassed for selection for the Lions tour of Australia.

During his career Mark sometimes courted controversy,

none more so than the furore that arose as a result of the decision of ten leading Welsh players to accept an invitation from the South African Rugby Union to join a world squad to play a number of games there to celebrate the Union's centenary in the summer of 1989. Owing to the fact that playing rugby in South Africa at the time was a politically sensitive issue, the tour arrangements were made in secret and publicity stifled to the extent that all negotiations were conducted without consultation with the WRU. However, news of the involvement of Welsh players, and at least one official, soon became public, leading to the resignation of the WRU president, Clive Rowlands and the secretary, David East.

In view of the disquiet that arose as a result of the tour the WRU ordered Vernon Pugh QC, later to become chairman of the IRB, to conduct an enquiry into the whole affair. Although no individual was compelled to contribute, Mark agreed to answer Vernon Pugh's questions and denied receiving any payment for taking part in the South African celebratory matches but later confessed that he had lied in that respect. In that 'amateur' era he had received £35,000 for his involvement, which had been paid into a secret bank account in Luxembourg. Periodically he drew on that account by making trips to London to meet a South African businessman who would provide him with the required cash. Mark also admitted that in 1983, as a budding star, he had participated in the centenary celebrations of Western Province in South Africa for the sum of £700.

Ring regained his place in the Wales team for the 1989–90 and 1990–1 Five Nations Championship and toured Namibia with his country in the summer of 1990.

However twelve months later he was omitted from the party to tour Australia by the coach Ron Waldron, with whom he had a fractious relationship, since it was thought his suspect knees would not be able to withstand the strain of playing on the hard grounds 'down under'. The tour was a disaster, Ron Waldron resigned and Alan Davies was appointed national coach in advance of the 1991 World Cup.

At the earliest opportunity Mark informed him that he would like to be considered for the outside-half position in the Wales team in their Pool matches, to be played in Cardiff. However a month prior to the start of the tournament he was forced to undergo surgery to try and rectify a cartilage problem in his right knee. Yet, despite his inability to train during the preparatory period, he was selected for each of those Pool games. With his knee heavily strapped, he gave the appearance of not being fit enough for such a demanding competition and was part of a generally disappointing performance which saw Wales make an early exit from the 1991 World Cup.

Mark never played for Wales again, although he continued to play club rugby, with Cardiff and then, briefly, for Pontypool once again. He left the Gwent club under a cloud two years later having been accused by the committee of allegedly misappropriating funds, an accusation which he strenuously denied and which led to Bobby Windsor resigning from the committee in protest at its decision to part company with their fly-half. He returned to Cardiff as a player and appeared in the 1996 Heineken Cup final against Toulouse. However, at the age of 33, having scored 94 tries in 262 appearances, he left to become player-coach at West Hartlepool from where he joined Penzance and Newlyn in a similar role.

With his playing days having come to an end he returned to Cardiff to work briefly for the Capital Rugby Community Development Scheme whilst also undertaking duties as the backs coach with Cardiff Rugby Club under the direction of Terry Holmes. When those positions were terminated he had further spells as coach at Caerphilly, Tetbury, with the Old Crescent Club in Ireland, and with Cross Keys. He has recently joined the staff at Cardiff Blues as a skills coach.

COLIN STEPHENS

HAVING EXCELLED AT outside-half at Ysgol y Strade, Llanelli and as a member of the Welsh Schools team Colin Stephens was first introduced to senior rugby with the Felinfoel club. Whilst still a teenager he was selected to play for Llanelli and benefited in those early days from the influence of Jonathan Davies who had moved to Stradey Park from Neath. He was cast in the Bennett 'jinking' mould and attributed much of his success at Llanelli to the advice he received from 'Benny' at club training sessions. Colin was noted for his impressive turn of speed, his ability to move the ball quickly and effectively through his hands, his elusiveness and his prodigious kicking prowess. His selection for his first senior cap at the age of 22, in January 1992 against Ireland in Dublin, came as a surprise to many rugby followers for, with Neil Jenkins being chosen to play for Wales in the centre for the first time in that game, it had been expected that Adrian Davies would fill the fly-half position.

Colin was the eighth player to be tried in that position since Jonathan Davies' last appearance in December 1988. In that respect he was unfortunate to be called to the international stage at a time when Wales were experiencing a very unsettled period. Despite an encouraging performance on his debut, during which he contributed a drop-goal in a Wales victory by 16–15, the team was heavily criticised following their subsequent defeat against France and a 24–0 drubbing by England. Colin bore the brunt of that criticism and he was the only Welsh back who was dropped for the last Championship match of that season against Scotland.

Two aspects of his game which were highlighted during those disappointing Wales performances, and which were generally recognised as weaknesses in his overall play during his career, were his defensive frailties, particularly in the tackle, and a distinctive lack of confidence when his team were under pressure. However, due to the fact that Neil Jenkins was suspended and that other contenders for the fly-half spot were experiencing injury problems, Colin was recalled to the Wales team during the following autumn to play in an uncapped match against Italy in Cardiff. Despite his demise at international level, he had been playing well for the Scarlets as indicated by his record-breaking 39-point haul in one game against Newport in September 1992. Wales beat Italy by 43–12, with Colin making a significant contribution with one try and four conversions, and despite some reservations as to the quality of the Wales performance, it was considered an useful exercise for the home team in preparation for their encounter against Australia six weeks later.

Immediately prior to that game against Australia he had given two impressive performances. Brought into the Wales B team against the tourists as a result of an injury to Neil Jenkins, he played with great authority, with his running in broken play being particularly effective. Then, one week before the Wales v Australia match he produced a match-winning performance against the Wallabies for Llanelli at Stradey in a memorable victory. Having engineered a try for Ieuan Evans under the posts following a magical dummy with Simon Davies, Colin converted to make the score 9–7 to the visitors. Then, in a dramatic climax to the game, he sealed a late Scarlets victory by 13–9 with two late and crucial drop-goals.

With Neil Jenkins still suffering from damaged ankle ligaments, Colin was once again recalled to the Wales team to face Australia one week later, in the hope he would be able to reproduce the kind of performance that toppled the Wallabies at Stradey. Unfortunately, he was given little opportunity to show his talents as Wales were well beaten by 23–6. It was his last appearance in a Welsh jersey and his loss of form and confidence saw him also lose favour with the Scarlets supporters and the club's selectors. In 1993 he joined Leeds Rugby Club and went on, in due course, to play for Yorkshire, Sedgley Park, Morley and Huddersfield. He also became assistant coach at Sedgley Park, took charge of the Academy with Leeds Tykes and in 2004 was appointed director of rugby at Leeds Metropolitan University, a position he still holds. In 2011 he also became director of rugby at Bradford and Bingley RFC, in Division Three of the English National League (a position currently held by Henry Paul). Colin is also a talented cricketer and, at one stage in his career, contemplated taking up the sport professionally. While at Llanelli he played cricket for Wales and Glamorgan Seconds, primarily as a quick bowler.

ALUN THOMAS

A NATIVE OF Cwmafan Alun Gruffydd Thomas was capped for the Welsh Secondary Schools XV just after World War II when a pupil at Port Talbot County School. He then studied at UCW Aberystwyth and played for the College First XV and the newly-founded Aberystwyth Rugby Club. His favoured position was outside-half and he started his first-class career playing there with Swansea Rugby Club, although he also appeared for them at centre. Having already been selected for Welsh trial matches, he joined Cardiff, where Cliff Morgan was soon to be established as the regular fly-half, at the start of the 1950–1 season. Cliff later admitted that his cause was helped by the fact that the Arms Park selectors deemed Alun to be a better centre than outside-half.

Indeed, just over two years later, Alun won his first cap as a centre against England at Twickenham but in rather acrimonious circumstances. At midnight on the Friday prior to the game, his colleague at Cardiff, Dr Jack Matthews, received a telephone call asking him to come to Twickenham on the Saturday morning since he would be required to play in place of Bleddyn Williams who had withdrawn because of injury. Dr Jack rushed up to London and having arrived in the dressing room learned that, following a hastily convened meeting in the changing room toilets, the selectors had decided to play Alun, the official travelling reserve, in the centre instead of him. Jack was naturally extremely annoyed and informed the selectors, after winning 17 caps, that he never wished to be considered for selection for the Wales team again.

The visitors won the match by 8–6, with their three-quarter line often displaying deft handling skills. However the occasion was noteworthy for another reason. A capacity crowd saw the gates at Twickenham being closed with thousands of Welsh supporters having been denied entry. Consequently, that was the last 'pay as you enter' match between England and Wales to be played there. The fixture two years later was a ticket-only affair for the first time.

Alun's versatility, deceptive running, exceptional ball-handling skills and all-round footballing ability entailed that he merited selection in several positions in the Wales team. Indeed during his first five appearances he didn't play in the same position in any two consecutive matches, winning caps in the centre, on the wing and, on one occasion, having been selected instead of the injured Cliff Morgan, at outside-half for the game against France at St Helen's, Swansea in 1952. Of course, his selection for the fly-half position was a recognition also of his kicking talents, both in attack and in defence and, aided by a drop-goal from Alun, Wales won a disappointing game by 9–5 to achieve the Grand Slam. One of the highlights of his early career was playing in the Cardiff team on the occasion of their memorable victory, by 8–3, over the 1953 All Blacks. The quality of his passing and 'magnetic handling' was evident throughout, particularly during the three-quarter movements that led to both Cardiff tries.

As well as being selected for the Barbarians he won 13 caps for his country, wearing the red shirt for the last time at Stade Colombes in Paris in March 1955, when he scored an outstanding try and created a second. This was the first ever all-ticket match for France in front of a crowd of 62,000, which was a record at that time. Alun was dropped from the Wales team for the opening game of that Five Nations Championship in 1956 as well as the final game of the previous Championship. With a view to reviving his apparently ailing international career, and having played 82 games for Cardiff, he had joined the Llanelli club at the beginning of the 1954–5 season, believing that perhaps his best chance of getting back into the Wales team was by playing at full-back. However, his excellent form with his new club and the general appreciation of his play at Stradey led to his regaining his accustomed position of centre for the last three international matches of that season.

He recalled with fondness in later years the initial reluctance of some partisan Llanelli supporters to accept him to the Stradey fold. Perhaps their main bone of contention was that Alun had once played for Swansea, their arch rivals. Upon the newcomer's arrival there, one wag had no truck with the view that Alun's versatility as a player would bring untold benefits to Llanelli and declared that Alun Thomas was the worst "futility player" ever to appear in a Scarlets shirt! The fact that the new acquisition was married to a member of the Blyth family, who were pillars of the Swansea club, did nothing to facilitate his standing with some followers. However Mrs Thomas was soon to make a favourable impression, leading one supporter to remark the she was the best "Jackess" that he'd ever met!

Not only did Alun's re-introduction to the international

stage in 1955 see him play very well for Wales, it also led to his being selected to tour South Africa with the British Lions that summer. He was valued as someone who would be able to play in a number of positions but it was believed that he would play mainly at full-back, a further indication of his versatility. The tour was indeed a success with the Lions winning 19 of their 25 matches and performing creditably in the four Tests to draw the series 2–2. However, Alun was dogged by injury throughout and only appeared in five provincial matches, kicking six conversions and one penalty goal.

Upon his return home Alun, who worked as an oil company representative, became the Llanelli club secretary, which was the beginning of a very successful administrative career. He was elected to the WRU committee in 1962 and became a member of the Big Five in 1963, a position he held until 1968. In 1964 he was chosen as assistant manager of the Wales tour to South Africa, which was the first time the national team had toured abroad. Despite winning three provincial matches the team was convincingly beaten by Northern Transvaal and by the Springboks in the only Test match. Following that tour Alun returned home convinced that urgent reorganisation of the administration of rugby at home was required if Wales wished to compete against the leading rugby-playing countries.

In that connection he was instrumental in pressurising the WRU to recognise the importance of coaching and the appointment of professionals to that end. However there was considerable opposition to such developments amongst some die-hard members of the WRU and Alun played a key role in the debate that ensued. As chairman of the selection committee and of the coaching committee he engineered, in 1967, the appointment of Ray Williams as the first national coaching organiser and the selection of three honorary coaches to take charge of three regional representative sides. His ardent recommendation that a coach should be appointed to accompany the Wales team on its tour of Argentina in 1968 was rejected by the WRU and Alun felt obliged to resign his positions with the Union. Yet he was vindicated in due course when at the annual general meeting it was agreed to ask the general committee to reconsider its decision. As a result Clive Rowlands became the first official coach to be assigned to the Wales team when they went to Argentina later that year. The two Test matches played there were designated as unofficial, with one being drawn and the other resulting in a victory for the home team.

In 1974 Alun achieved perhaps the greatest honour of his rugby career when he was chosen as manager of the controversial Lions tour to South Africa. Despite objections to the tour by the Government and other bodies and prominent individuals, and protests by anti-apartheid demonstrators, the Lions undertook one of their most impressive tours ever. Alun and his management team deserve no little credit for the success of the 1974 Lions, as they won 21 of their matches, with one drawn game, breaking several records in the process. Playing an exciting brand of rugby which gained them many admirers, they won the first three Tests and drew the fourth, thus clinching a series in South Africa for the first time. It was, however, one of the most violent Lions tours ever and, in that context, the management team won the admiration of its players for refusing to accept capitulation as a response to the ultra-physical approach which was often displayed by the home teams.

From the outset it was observed that the opposition were usually intent on dominating the forward exchanges by virtue of their superior size and consequently on using physical intimidation, by fair means or foul, to try to gain the ascendancy. The players therefore were grateful to Alun and Syd Millar, the coach, for supporting their efforts to counter the Springboks' bullying tactics, particularly with regard to the '99' call that was sometimes uttered when one of the Lions was being put upon by the opposition. At that particular point all their players would wade into action against every Springbok within reach. This ploy was based on the premise that so many players would be fighting as a result of that plan of action that the referee would be unable to send anyone off!

During one such battle in the third Test, Gordon Brown, the Scottish second row, hit his opposite number, Johan de Bruyn, with such a heavy blow that the South African's glass eye shot out. As a result both teams and the referee crawled about in the mud to try and find the missing object, which they did in due course, whereupon a delighted de Bruyn popped the eye back in its socket and the game continued. Sadly Brown died from non-Hodgkin's lymphoma in 2001 at the age of 53 and shortly afterwards de Bruyn had the glass eye especially mounted in the form of a trophy which he presented to his former adversary's widow!

Alun was once again selected as a member of the Big Five in 1978. Ironically, having resigned ten years earlier over the WRU's reluctance to fully embrace the importance of coaching, he was now able to draw satisfaction at first hand from the manner in which the Union's official coaching policy was paying dividends. In 1985 he was elected president of the WRU and also served during the latter part of his life as an appeals' officer with the National Trust. He sadly died in 1991 at the age of 65. As an administrator, Welsh rugby is greatly indebted to his unstinting pursuit in the 1960s of the importance of adopting a formal coaching policy. As a player his talents were best described by Cliff Morgan, who called him "a class act!"

ARWEL THOMAS

A NATIVE OF Trebanos in the Swansea Valley, Arwel was a tremendously gifted outside-half who, like Mark Ring, was able to entertain, enthral, excite and exasperate, sometimes in the same game! He first appeared for Wales shortly after Kevin Bowering became the national coach, who stated on the occasion of his appointment that he wished to "put the smile back on Welsh faces". He believed that Arwel was well equipped to do just that and that his creative abilities would provide the Wales three-quarter line with a cutting edge that had been lacking for some time. He stated that the young outside-half "had a responsibility and a maturity as well as an unpredictability and spontaneity that may be a catalyst for others". Arwel won the first of his 23 caps (four of which were as a replacement) against Italy in 1996, due to the fact that the incumbent fly-half, Neil Jenkins, was injured. That was the beginning of a prolonged debate, as had been the case over the years with regard to other contenders for the number ten position in the Wales team, concerning the merits of both Arwel and Neil.

The latter's attributes have been discussed earlier and despite some similarities, for example their particular match-winning abilities, they possessed contrasting styles. The words flair and vision could be applied to Arwel as he always sought to entertain with his adventurous, intuitive play. Such play was, of course, sometimes unpredictable which led Barry John to comment, "When Arwel has the ball a try is always likely. The trouble is you can't be sure at which end!" He was a deceptive runner whose handling and passing skills were particularly good. He was a master at choosing effective running angles and of inducing penetrative contributions from supporting players. For such a diminutive player, just 5' 9" and weighing barely 11 stone when he first played for Wales, he possessed a powerful boot, although his ability to manage a game was sometimes called into question.

His introduction to international rugby was promising. He had been an influential member of the Wales A team that had won the Grand Slam, scoring 77 points in four games. In that first senior international against Italy in Cardiff, he showed commendable touches and scored 16 of the home team's points, in a victory by 31–26, although lacking the experience to exercise his control over the game. Perhaps the most pleasing aspect of the performance was the fact that, in keeping with Kevin Bowering's philosophy of playing entertaining rugby, half the team were under 23 years old, with five being capped for the first time. The next game away to England in the Five Nations Championship saw Arwel display his precocious approach for the first time at international level. Following the award of a penalty to Wales, within goal-kicking distance, the England team turned around and retreated towards their try-line in anticipation of a fairly easy attempt at goal from Arwel. He rapidly assessed the resultant lack of cover in the England defensive line-up, took a quick tap-penalty, moved the ball smartly to see it being passed speedily through the hands of two supporting players for Hemi Taylor to crash over for a try. At the time Arwel's vision for such an inexperienced player at that level was widely commended.

© Getty Images

Defensively he was sometimes found wanting and despite being generally composed under pressure he could be suspect in the tackle area. Although not a shirker in that respect, his fragile stature often led to his being dismissively cast aside by rampaging opponents. For example after Wales were comprehensively beaten by

South Africa in 1998, by 98–13 (when Arwel scored all of his country's points, including a try) a press report stated that in defence 'he was like a feather caught up in a gale'. He was sometimes targeted by the opposition, as in the defeat against Ireland at Landsdowne Road in 1996 when Arwel gained his fourth cap. The Irish later admitted that they had earmarked him for the 'brown trouser treatment' early in that game, which entailed kicking the ball high into the air in his direction and, as he gathered, piling in forcefully on top of him. Arwel was left decidedly groggy after that encounter. He did not know where he was when he got up and although passed fit to continue by the team doctor he had, by his own admission, a nightmare of a match from then on. He dropped a few passes, missed some kicks at goal and two wayward attempted clearance kicks led to Irish tries.

He was later heavily criticised as a result and lost his place in the Wales team. He would always take such judgement to heart which would often undermine his confidence yet there was no denying his physical commitment on the field which belied his juvenile appearance. That was amply and unexpectedly illustrated in the game against France at Parc des Princes in 1997. Having been struck a glancing blow to the face by Philippe Carbonneau, the France scrum-half, during loose play, Arwel uncharacteristically retaliated with one of the best punches ever seen at the stadium, to leave his opponent prostrate on the ground and needing attention from the trainer!

Following that disappointing display against Ireland, Arwel was not selected for Wales for the next seven international matches, until he replaced an injured Jonathan Davies for the game against South Africa in

December 1996. However his third game back, against Scotland in January 1997, was one of his most memorable in the red shirt when he was at his mercurial best. He regularly took on his opponents and seemed to be able to rip through their defence at will. He had a hand in the three tries which Wales scored during a six-minute spell, getting one himself following a 50-metre dash for the line. In the process of crossing he memorably caused some concern amongst his supporters as he managed to stop and touch down with only a yard to spare before reaching the dead-ball line. Scotland, after being ahead by 16–10 at one point, were well beaten by 34–19, with their captain, Rob Wainright, a member of the home team's back row that had been given a torrid time by Arwel, remarking after the match, "We didn't have a clue what he would do next!"

Later that year in the victory over Romania by 70–21, Arwel scored 23 points, including two tries, to become at that time the highest ever try-scorer for a Welsh outside-half. However, with the departure of Kevin Bowering in 1998, Arwel's selection for the national team for the next three years was sporadic. Yet, despite Graham Henry's preference for physicality in his players (a feature which saw Shane Williams being ignored for a period) the national coach surprisingly recalled Arwel to the Wales side to face Samoa and then the USA in November 2000. He had been playing well for Swansea in the Heineken Cup, while Neil Jenkins was not having a particularly good season with Cardiff and there had been considerable public acclaim for Arwel's recall to the national team.

He bagged a tally of 35 points for the two games in question, which included a try in the second match which

Henry described as "a gem". Yet he dropped him for the next game against South Africa having described his overall performance in the previous two games as merely "adequate". But after 60 minutes of the game against the Springboks, Arwel replaced Neil Jenkins who up until that point had been playing quite well. Doubtless the substitute, particularly in the light of Henry's recent morale-sapping comment, felt under a great deal of pressure and consequently had one of his more disappointing games for Wales. He failed to convert a fairly easy penalty and two attempted drop-goals, took a poor drop out which led to a Springbok try and gave a penalty away from which the visitors got another three points. It was Arwel's final appearance in a Wales jersey, having scored 216 points, comprising 12 tries, 32 penalties and 30 conversions.

As a young man he was selected for the Wales Youth team and played for Trebanos Rugby Club. He had played one game for Swansea Rugby Club before opting to join Neath during the 1994–5 season. At the Gnoll his early promise led many supporters to believe that the Club had found a worthy successor to Jonathan Davies. However such early pressure doubtless had some influence on Arwel's decision to join Bristol Rugby Club for the 1995–6 season which was also facilitated to some extent by the fact that he was by that time a student at Filton College, Bristol. Indeed his first four caps for Wales were won while he played for Bristol.

His remaining Welsh appearances were as a Swansea player, and during his seven years with the club he scored 1,963 points, a tally which included 40 tries, 328 conversions, 338 penalties and 31 drop-goals. Following brief interludes with Pau, in France (he had previously turned down an offer to join Toulouse in 1999), Llanelli, Llandovery (just one game) and Harlequins, he returned to Neath in 2005. He announced his retirement at the end of the 2007–8 season, only to change his mind later and captain Neath for the 2009–10 season. He finally retired having score 781 points with the Gnoll side, comprising 13 tries, 148 conversions, 131 penalties and nine drop-goals. During 2012–13 he was player-coach with Birchgrove Rugby Club, in Division Four of the SWALEC League.

In February 1997 Arwel played in the Wales team that lost by 27–22 to France at Parc des Princes. Nevertheless, even in defeat Arwel's enterprise often drew accolades from knowledgeable rugby critics and, after that particular game, Serge Blanco, a former French rugby star who was also renowned for his exciting and adventurous play, predicted that Arwel would have a major contribution to make to the Wales team in the future, describing him as "a very, very fine player". Maybe the arrival of the professional era and the increased importance attributed to bulk and muscle was not conducive to seeing Arwel verify the first part of Blanco's declaration. However there is no denying the verity of the second part.

MALCOLM THOMAS

O N THE DAY that Malcolm Campbell broke the
world land speed record in 1929, a baby boy was
born to Mr and Mrs Thomas in Machen, near Newport.
To commemorate the occasion they named their son
Malcolm Campbell, after the celebrated motor pioneer,
and his connection with land speed records ended with
the name, yet he did go on to break records on the rugby
field and to frequently exhibit attributes such as power and
speed. In addition to his having a mastery of basic rugby
skills, versatility and dependability became synonymous
with the name of Malcolm Thomas. Although capped
27 times by Wales he appeared just once in the outside-
half position, in his final game in Paris in 1959. Twenty-
one of his appearances in the red jersey were as a centre
whilst he was chosen to play on the wing on five other
occasions. During his time in the Welsh team he made
a significant contribution to its success in winning two
Grand Slams, two Triple Crowns and three Five Nations
Championships.

He played his first game for Newport Rugby Club as a
16 year old in 1946 while still a pupil at Bassaleg Grammar
School. He represented the Welsh Secondary Schools at
both rugby and cricket and went on to play rugby for
Newport on 280 occasions. In the early 1950s the club
had one of the strongest sides in Wales with exciting
players such as Ken Jones and Roy Burnett forming part
of a scintillating three-quarter line alongside Malcolm.
During his career with the Black and Ambers he scored

297 points, which included 65 tries, four drop-goals, 16 penalties and 21 conversions.

Upon leaving school he became a student at Caerleon Training College with a view to becoming a teacher, from where he enlisted to become an instructor lieutenant in the Royal Navy. He had by then been capped three times by Wales as a Newport player, but for the next two seasons he turned out for Devonport Services in Cornwall, while serving with the Navy. The club was based at Plymouth, drawing its players from the Armed Forces, and at that time had regular fixtures with leading British rugby clubs. It was as a Devonport player that he was selected for his fourth game in the red jersey, on the left wing against Ireland in Belfast, on 11 March 1950, an occasion which established Malcolm as one of the future stars of Welsh rugby. With the score at 3–3, and with just a few minutes of the game remaining and Ireland under pressure in their own 22 area, he received the ball some 20 metres from the line and hurtled over to touch down in the corner, taking two defenders and the corner flag with him. That score meant that Wales had won their first Triple Crown for 39 years. The achievement was overshadowed however by a tragic air accident the following day when a plane carrying supporters back to Cardiff from Ireland crashed at Llandow, killing 80 passengers and crew. Among the dead was a brother of Roy Burnett, Malcolm's colleague in the Newport team.

That particular score by Thomas against Ireland encapsulated the characteristics with which his play became associated throughout his career, namely a safe pair of hands, a strong outside burst at speed and a hand-off like a sledgehammer, facilitated by his sturdy 5' 10" and

13 stone 10 pounds build, which kept potential tacklers at bay. Accompanied by an ability to link smoothly with other players around him and powerful determination in the tackle, such assets were instrumental in establishing Malcolm as a one of the most reliable of the Welsh backs over a remarkable period of ten years. He was also an excellent tactical kicker and was frequently called upon by club and country to undertake place-kicking duties.

He won his first 15 caps consecutively before losing his place in 1953 to Alun Thomas. A broken leg sustained in a club trial match and the consequent comeback trail kept him out of the national reckoning for a while, but he returned to the Wales fold in 1956 and played another twelve times until his retirement in 1959. While with Devonport Services he represented Cornwall and captained the Navy, the youngest player ever to do so. He led his team to victory in the Inter-Services Championship and also skippered the combined Army and Navy team. He was captain of Newport for three seasons (during which period they won the Welsh Club Championship), as well as leading Monmouthshire (who won the Welsh Counties Championship under his captaincy) and the Barbarians, and represented Newport against South Africa (1952), New Zealand (1954) and Australia (1957). At the height of his success he turned down an offer of £5,000 to join Leeds Rugby League Club.

He was also honoured with the captaincy of the Welsh team for two games, against England and Scotland in the 1957 Five Nations Championship. Perhaps his most notable achievement was being selected to tour with the British Lions on two occasions, firstly to New Zealand and Australia in 1950, when, at the age of 19 he was the youngest member of the party (until Lewis Jones joined at a later date as a replacement). Although the Lions lost the Test series, the back division, of which Malcolm was an integral and outstanding part, made a distinct impression.

In 1958 Newport wanted Malcolm Thomas to play at outside-half where, once again, he excelled and when he played for Wales against France in 1958 there were three club fly-halves in the team: Malcolm, along with his partner in the centre, Carwyn James of Llanelli, and Cliff Morgan, the Cardiff outside-half, who was representing his country for the last time. Cliff was replaced the following season by Cliff Ashton, of Aberavon, who was unavailable for the final game in Paris against France. As a result of his success in that position with Newport, the selectors chose Malcolm as the fly-half for that game, his first appearance for his country that season. Despite the fact that Wales lost by 11–3, he obviously did enough to persuade the Lions selectors that he deserved to tour with them to New Zealand and Australia later that year.

On that occasion he was the oldest playing member of the party at the age of 29. During that second tour, an indication of his adaptable and indispensable talents was perhaps the fact that he played in every position behind the scrum except scrum-half. In the provincial game against a Combined XV at Blenheim, he beat the individual scoring record for a Lions tour that he himself had established against Nelson in 1950, by getting 25 points, comprising eight conversions and three penalties, thus underlining his invaluable contribution to the tour. It was considerably shorter than Malcolm's first Lions trip in 1950, which was undertaken by sea and which entailed being away from home for six months, whereas in 1959 the tour party had the luxury of travelling by aeroplane to their destination and back. In all he scored 152 points for the Lions and played in four Test matches and upon his return from his second tour 'down under' Malcolm announced his retirement from rugby.

Having initially taken a teaching post in Cardiff upon leaving the Navy, he decided that his future lay in industry and in particular the paper industry. He moved eventually to Buckinghamshire and became a highly successful businessman. In 1973 he was made managing director of the Reid Group Packaging Division while holding a number of other non-executive directorships and in 1993 he was appointed group chairman of Hornby Hobbies. For some years he reported on rugby for the *Sunday Telegraph*.

Malcolm had always been an all-round sportsman. He played cricket for Cornwall in the 1951 Minor Counties Championship, making his debut, alongside his Wales and Devonport colleague, Lewis Jones, against a Surrey Second XI at the Oval, where he scored 56 and impressed with his fast-medium bowling. In six innings in the competition he scored 158 runs and on his retirement from rugby he maintained his interest in cricket by playing at club level. He was also a single-figure handicap golfer. He died in 2012, in Beaconsfield, Buckinghamshire, at the age of 82 having been predeceased by his wife in 1997.

PAUL TURNER

Having played outside-half at first-class level for many years for Newbridge and Newport Paul Turner was finally selected for his country at the comparatively mature age of 30 years old. Some critics believed that he had been denied recognition in international rugby because of his inclination to engage in adventurous play, on occasions when more prudent action would have served his team better. Sometimes his seemingly overconfident approach would lead to errors of judgement which resulted in his team being put under pressure. The national selectors would have allegedly viewed that particular tendency as a weakness in his play, and his selection to appear on the international stage as too great a risk. Nevertheless it could not be denied that he was blessed with considerable flair and that many rugby followers were enamoured of his exciting approach to the game. In that respect his skills were also recognised by the Barbarians.

Notwithstanding his enterprising running talents, perhaps his greatest attribute was his mastery of all forms of kicking and in that respect he was able to use either foot with equal dexterity and apparent effortlessness. His deceptively long and accurate punts, with the screw-kick forming an essential and effective part of his armoury, could be invaluable in relieving pressure on his team's defence, as was his decisive tactical kicking in attack. In addition his skills with the boot were primarily responsible for the substantial points aggregate which he amassed with the two sides noted above, setting a club record at Newbridge in the 1983–4 season with a total of 405 points for the season and similarly at Newport when he scored 442 points in 41 appearances in 1986–7.

When his days as a player at Rodney Parade came to an end in 1992 he was the club's all-time leading points scorer (a record which lasted until 2008) with a total of 992 points, comprising 22 tries, 251 conversions, 161 penalties and 24 drop-goals. He also scored 153 points while on tour with the club. Were it not for the fact that he played 13 games for London Welsh in 1987 and also returned to Newbridge, as captain, for that club's 1989–90 centenary season, his overall points total for Newport would have been much greater.

Nevertheless, it was as a Newbridge player that he won his three caps in 1989, the first ever of the club's backs to achieve that honour. Paul's initial appearance in the red shirt was, as a replacement for Paul Thorburn, in the full-back position, against Ireland at the Arms Park, which was followed by his selection as outside-half in the remaining Five Nations fixtures against France and England. The latter game provided Wales with their only victory in the Championship that season. With Jonathan Davies having joined Widnes the previous December, filling the outside-half position subsequently, for a time, caused the selectors many problems.

Having left Newbridge Comprehensive in 1977 to take employment as a civil servant, Paul began his senior rugby career with Crumlyn, before joining Pontypool for a brief period. In 1979 he moved to the Newbridge club and for 1983–4 and 1984–5 he was elected captain but then left for Rodney Parade. In his final season with Newport he served as player-coach and continued in that role with Sale Rugby Club from 1992–6. He was instrumental in establishing Sale during that period as a club that would compete at the highest level in the English Premiership, which would result in subsequent years in their winning the European Challenge Cup and the Premiership Championship.

After leaving Sale a series of coaching appointments followed, with Bedford (where he also continued as a player), Saracens, Rugby, Gloucester and Harlequins. In 2005 he joined Newport Dragons as head coach and became highly respected in his field, despite the difficulties of having to operate within a comparatively small budget. His efforts were recognised in 2010 when he was elected Magners League Coach of the Year. However, after six seasons, his tenure at Rodney Parade ended in acrimony. In the first instance he was forced by the club to apologise on the Newport Dragons website for unfairly criticising the WRU in an article in the *South Wales Argus*. Then, having been asked by a reporter at a press conference about his future with the Dragons in view of their recent poor results, Paul insisted, in an allegedly threatening manner, that the person concerned left the meeting. As a result of these incidents his employment with the Dragons came to an end by mutual agreement in February 2011.

Later that year he was engaged for one season as consultant attack and skills coach with London Wasps and in 2012, based in St Albans, he established the Paul Turner Elite Coaching Consultancy. During his coaching career he has often undertaken part-time engagements, for example he coached Hertfordshire to the final of the English County Championship and took up an appointment in 2012 as head coach with Amphill and District Rugby Club in Division Three of the English National League. Whereas his vision and creative talents as a player were greatly admired, his ability to convey such attributes to young players and various clubs has ensured that his services as a coach are widely appreciated.

DAVID WATKINS

WHEN SHANE WILLIAMS, towards the end of 2012, remarked that his house had started to shake when an earthquake struck the area where he was living in Japan, Mike Phillips tweeted that he must have dropped his wallet! It represented the latest in a series of references over the years to wallets and lucrative pay deals for rugby players. David Watkins, the former Newport fly-half, who was almost universally known as 'Dai' throughout his career, was the first person, in my personal experience, to have been subjected to such a comment. Having just signed, as a 25 year old, for Salford Rugby League Club in 1967, for a record fee of £16,000, he was advised by a wag on the terrace, upon his failure to tackle an opponent, to "'it 'im with your wallet instead!"

The remark was a reflection of the cynical reception he received from fans, players and sometimes referees at the outset of his rugby league career. There was a certain animosity, even from some fellow team-members, that a player from another code, who had no prior experience of their particular game, was being paid a small fortune compared to that which native league players were getting. Indeed by comparison, Dai's own earnings until then, firstly as a management trainee in the local steelworks, then as a tyre depot manager, and finally as a representative of Forward Trust, a subsidiary of Midland Bank, paled into insignificance.

The game at that time was markedly more undisciplined

and in his first few years Dai was subjected to a great deal of dirty and brutal play from over-physical opponents. In some respects his diminutive build of 5' 6" and 10½ stone made him easy prey. During that early period he had his nose broken four times, suffered a double fracture of the jaw and several broken ribs, as a result of off-the-ball incidents, to the extent that he even considered turning his back on rugby league! In one match, he appealed to the referee for some protection from the rough treatment being handed out by his opponents. To his dismay the referee's response was that he had been paid enough to be able to look after himself!

However his innate perseverance, courage and sheer ability ensured that he did not succumb to the rigours of rugby league at the time and that he developed to become one of the greatest three-quarters that the 13-man game had ever seen. He was a record points scorer for Salford, with 2,907 points, having played for them for 13 seasons in 405 games as fly-half, centre and full-back. Between 1971–4 he appeared in a record 140 consecutive matches (which in itself is testimony to his remarkable durability) and scored in a record 92 of them. He kicked a world record 221 goals in 1973–4 and led his club to numerous honours. He continued to excel for one season with Swinton Rugby League Club after leaving Salford. He was selected for Great Britain on six occasions and for the Wales rugby league team in 16 matches. He also captained both teams and served as the Great Britain coach in the 1977 World Cup.

David Watkins was first introduced to the activities of rugby league in the early 1960s while still a teenager. He had just represented Wales Youth against France when three representatives of the St Helens club called at his parents' home in Blaina and opened a case containing £5,000, which would be Dai's if he signed for their club. His father, whilst still in shock at the sight of so much money on the table, wanted him to put pen to paper immediately but his wife soon put paid to any aspirations he and her son might have had on that score by insisting that David was too young to 'go north' to live on his own! An identical scenario had been enacted some years previously in a kitchen in Trebanog when scouts came in pursuit of Cliff Morgan!

In an area such as the Gwent Valleys it was natural that Dai took an early interest in rugby, even though other sports had their appeal. He enjoyed playing soccer, he was an excellent cricketer and was later a member of the Welsh AAA relay team. As a schoolboy he played local representative rugby as a scrum-half because the fly-half position had been claimed by Arthur Lewis who went on to play centre for Ebbw Vale, Wales and the British Lions. Dai's dedication in those early days is perhaps illustrated by the fact that, although a natural right-footer, he would spend hours punting a rugby ball up against a local coal tip with his left boot. Each effort would result in the ball rolling back down for him to gather and kick again.

He first made a name for himself as an outside-half with the local Cwmcelyn Youth team which he captained during the 1959–60 season and from which he progressed to play for Monmouthshire Youth. In due course he was selected for Wales Youth, whom he represented on six occasions over two years. In those days youth players were permitted to play four games of senior rugby each season and in this connection he turned out for Blaina,

Abertillery, Ebbw Vale and Pontypool, before making a successful request to appear in pre-season trials with Newport in 1961.

He made an immediate impression and was selected for the first team. Within a few months he'd taken part in the first and second Welsh trials and he represented his country at Under 23 level. Following his appearance in the final Welsh trial in the autumn of 1962, he won his first senior cap against England in January 1963. His scrum-half partner on the day was Clive Rowlands, who was also making his first appearance for his country and who had the rare distinction of being made captain on the occasion of his debut. They played together for Wales for three seasons and 14 consecutive matches, with Clive acting as skipper in every one, a run which also included games against the touring All Blacks and the Springboks in Durban.

Dai played 21 times for Wales but it took him a little time to establish himself in the Welsh team as the outstanding player he became. He was a scintillating runner with the ball in hand, but critics in the early days pointed to his tendency at times to run too far, in an attempt to beat too many defenders, which resulted in his losing touch with colleagues around him. With increasingly more experience at international level, he became more disciplined in his approach, yet without sacrificing his explosive acceleration and defence-splitting sidesteps which were such an essential part of his game and which were exemplified in the magnificent solo try he scored against Ireland in 1964. To these qualities he added a masterful kicking repertoire, both in terms of tactical punting and points scoring, and spirited covering in defence. Even in the most dire conditions, such as the mud-patch that was the Cardiff Arms Park pitch for the game against Scotland in 1966, Dai was able to work his magic so effectively, as he frequently danced his way through the opposition defence, while those about him struggled and floundered. In 1997 Cliff Morgan described that performance as "The best game I think I've ever seen a fly-half play for his country."

He played for Newport, whom he skippered from 1964–7, on 202 occasions over a period of six seasons, scoring 288 points (165 of which were from 55 drop-goals). One of his great achievements at club level was his contribution in the defeat, by 3–0, of the 1963 All Blacks by Newport as result of a drop-goal by John Uzzell, which was the culmination of a sweeping move instigated by Dai. That was the visitors' only defeat on their 36-match tour of the British Isles. In keeping with his particular skills, he was an exceptional seven-a-side player and in that context he never played in a losing Newport side.

Having appeared in 18 consecutive games for Wales he was selected to tour Australia and New Zealand with the British Lions in 1966. He played at outside-half in all six Tests, at the expense of the much vaunted Irishman, Mike Gibson, who was selected at centre and who had told Dai privately that perhaps he should have been selected instead of the Gwent man, since he was the better fly-half! Apart from showing outstanding form in some of the provincial games, Dai's standing was considerably increased by his being chosen to captain two of the Tests against the All Blacks. This was a reflection not only of the respect he held as an inspirational leader, but of his acquired maturity which enabled him to read and manage a game effectively.

His particular achievements as captain are also illustrated by the fact that he is the only player to have captained Great Britain at rugby union and rugby league.

The tour on the whole was a great disappointment, in that the four Tests and four provincial games were lost in New Zealand. One of the major talking points was the blow which the mighty Colin Meads landed on Dai who, having been late-tackled by the Kiwi, got up and swore at him. For his pains the Lions outside-half received a punch in the mouth which laid him out cold and eventually required six stitches. The referee was apparently 'unsighted', so Meads went unpunished and although the 6' 3" and 16½ stone second row apologised some years later, he claimed that he had acted 'in self-defence'! While Dai had delighted the southern hemisphere crowds with his adventurous outlook, the media in New Zealand, obsessed as they were in those days with the glorification of robust and storming forward play, were unimpressed with the spontaneity with which he played. Yet he was described by his manager, Des O'Brien, as "probably the most outstanding rugby player with the team" and was one of the few Lions players to return home with an enhanced reputation.

Yet, to the amazement of rugby followers, for the next Wales game against Australia in the autumn of the 1966–7 season, the selectors chose Barry John at outside-half, who was winning his first cap, even though Dai had been informed personally by three of the five selectors that they had cast their vote for him! However, one of the first congratulatory telegrams that Barry received was from the man that he had deposed. The decision became the subject of national debate and, although Barry retained his place for the first two matches of 1967, Dai was recalled for the remaining three Five Nations matches and made captain! The fickleness of the selection process was no doubt an influential factor in his decision to join Salford Rugby League Club later that year.

He was probably the first player to 'go north' without incurring the wholesale rancour of the Union establishment in Wales. On his departure he received a letter from the secretary of the WRU, Bill Clements, thanking him for his valuable contribution and complementing him for being a great credit to Wales on and off the field. Before appearing for Salford against Castleford in the 1967 rugby league Challenge Cup final, Dai received a telegram from Rees Stephens, one of the Welsh selectors, wishing him well for the game. Yet there were instances of his being treated as some kind of rugby league pariah when he returned to Wales. For example, having accepted an invitation to form part of a BBC commentary team for a Cardiff v Llanelli game at the Arms Park, Dai was regrettably informed by the producer a few hours before kick-off that his press pass had inexplicably been withdrawn!

Having retired from league rugby Dai returned to Gwent and maintained an active interest in both codes. He served as managing director of the Cardiff Blue Dragons rugby league team and was president of the Celtic Crusaders. He also became team manager, chairman and later president of Newport Rugby Club and was awarded the MBE for his services to rugby. The celebrated England and British Lions outside-half, Richard Sharp, who opposed Dai on the occasion of his international debut in 1963, later wrote: "Passing, kicking, running and handling, tackling and speed of thought and action are all vital to the successful outside-half. The one man who has all these attributes and who must surely be the best fly-half the world has known is David Watkins, of Newport."

BLEDDYN WILLIAMS

For someone who was known as the 'Prince of Centres', due to his being one of the greatest players ever to appear in that position, Bleddyn Llewellyn Williams, rather surprisingly perhaps, won his first cap for Wales against England in January 1947 as a fly-half. However, it was to be the only time that he played there for his country. Having suffered a muscle injury during the opening minutes and having consequently been hounded and restricted by the opposing breakaway forwards, Bleddyn had a disappointing debut. For the next match against Scotland he was chosen in his more accustomed left-centre position (he always preferred the midfield combination of left/right rather than inside/outside) and for the next few years, except when prevented by injury, he became an automatic selection there.

As a 14 year old in the Cardiff Schoolboys team his favoured position was fly-half yet he was selected for the Welsh Schoolboys team that defeated England by 29–0 as a full-back. Some months later he was awarded a scholarship by Rydal School (upon the recommendation of a distinguished former pupil, Wilf Wooller) where he continued to excel as an outside-half. Indeed, before leaving school at the age of 18 to join the RAF, he had already turned out occasionally for the Cardiff club.

During the Second World War he trained as a pilot and was actively involved as a glider pilot over the Rhine. He nevertheless managed to take part in numerous wartime representative rugby matches and soon began making a name for himself as a player of great quality, both at fly-half and as a centre. For when playing for Wales in service internationals he sometimes appeared alongside the established Wales international outside-half, Willie Davies, which meant that a place was found for Bleddyn in the centre.

Upon the resumption of post-war first-class fixtures, he joined Cardiff (as did all of his seven brothers at various times) for the 1945–6 season. He played in midfield, alongside Jack Matthews and outside Billy Cleaver, in an extremely talented Black and Blues three-quarter line. However, the following season, he moved to fly-half, with Cleaver and Matthews taking up the centre positions. This came about because Bleddyn liked the idea of playing outside-half and because such a change could be conveniently accommodated due to the versatility of that particular trio. The arrangement seemed to work for a number of games, including a series of Welsh trials, and indeed that particular formation took the field for Wales on the occasion of Bleddyn's first cap.

However, its failure to excel on the day not only led the Welsh selectors to abandon the newly-formed plan but also caused the Cardiff club to re-think its strategy, with the result that Bleddyn was duly restored to the centre berth. For the next eight years he established himself as one of the most complete and exciting rugby players ever to have played the game. In 283 games for Cardiff he scored 185 tries and, in 1947–8, broke the club record for the highest number of tries in a season when he crossed 41 times. Prior to the last game he had scored 37 tries but crowned a magnificent season by getting four tries in that final encounter with Gloucester. In his typically modest way he maintained that he succeeded in obtaining the required tries to break the record because his team-mates insisted on giving him scoring passes when they could very well have touched down themselves!

Although dogged by injury in 1950 and 1952, his career as a Wales player was just as illustrious. In 22 matches for his country he scored seven tries and captained the team on five victorious occasions. He appeared in five of the six Test matches (missing the first against the All Blacks through injury) played by the British Lions in New Zealand and Australia in 1950 and during that tour scored 13 tries in 20 games, while confirming his reputation as a centre of the highest class. Among his most notable achievements were leading Cardiff and then Wales to memorable wins against the touring All Blacks in 1953. During those encounters he displayed talents beyond those which were required as a player. For it was generally considered that the victories in question were due in no small part to the tactics which Bleddyn, as captain, had formulated for his teams and which resulted from his acute analysis of the tourists' playing patterns.

It is perhaps unfortunate that rugby followers had been deprived of bearing witness to his boundless talent for such a lengthy period during the war years. However, it could be argued that after emerging on to the first-class rugby stage in 1946, he was well on the way to becoming a 'complete' centre, possessing also attributes which would have seen him excel at outside-half. He was sturdily built, being 5' 10" tall and weighing 13½ stone, yet was very quick off the mark. He was a superb passer of the ball, with immaculate timing when feeding others, to the extent that he would often take two or three prospective opposition tacklers out of the game by virtue of the precision of his pass. Testimony to this particular skill is the fact that, despite his being a prolific try-scorer himself, he was even more influential in the way he would frequently send his wingers on a clear path to the line. He claims that this particular virtue was instilled in him as a result of a comment by his headmaster at Rydal who, on one occasion, having witnessed Bleddyn beating four men to score a try, kindly suggested to him that he should have passed to his wing who would not have needed to beat anyone to touch down!

He possessed a devastating sidestep off either foot but his most telling attacking weapon was the jink. The uninitiated would perhaps enquire as to the difference between these two seemingly identical talents and, with regard to Bleddyn Williams in particular, the authors of *Fields of Praise* provide the answer:

> The sidestep is done at speed, performed as Gerald Davies would breathtakingly demonstrate, without any perceptible lessening of pace. Its essence is timing. The jink, Bleddyn's jink, was a more static affair. It meant coming almost to a temporary halt. Its essence was positional and psychological, whereby one drew the opponent into knowing the jink was coming, though when it did come he was helpless to do anything about it. The thousands who thronged to see Cardiff play went to see Bleddyn's rippling jink.

To complement his evasive running skills Bleddyn would always expound the merits of carrying the ball before him in both hands at all times so that, by lowering his shoulder while in full flight, and leaning in a particular direction he could wrong-foot any prospective tackler. He was a great advocate of the scissors movement and in practice would take time to instruct his fellow three-quarters at Cardiff in the essentials of that particular art. He was also an excellent kicker of the ball from the hands, in attack as well as in defence. Cliff Morgan, a contemporary of his in the Cardiff and Wales team, compared his exemplary timing when exercising this particular skill with the boot to that which pertained to great golfers when striking the ball. Neither was he lacking in any way in the most basic of defensive arts, the tackle.

From his early days in first-class rugby Bleddyn attracted bids from rugby league clubs. In 1947, for example, Leeds sent their manager, the renowned Eddie Waring, to Cardiff with a cheque for £6,000, to try and tempt him to sign for them, which in current terms would have made Bleddyn a millionaire. He, of course, rejected all approaches of this kind, such was his love for the Union game. After retiring in 1955 he became rugby correspondent for *The People* and worked in broadcasting. He was also employed as regional marketing manager for Wimpey Construction and as an executive with the Steel Company of Wales. Bleddyn died in 2009 at the age of 86 years. The late W.O. Williams the celebrated Wales and British Lion forward, who played alongside and against Bleddyn on many occasions, wrote that he was the greatest footballer he had ever seen; indeed, he added, he was 'the greatest of the greats'. There are not many who would disagree with him.

BIBLIOGRAPHY

Newspapers:

Western Mail, South Wales Evening Post, South Wales Echo, South Wales Argus, Carmarthen Journal, Llanelli Star.

Books:

Bennett, Phil, *The Autobiography* (Willow, 2004).

Bevan, Alun Wyn, *Straeon o'r Strade* (Gomer, 2004).

—, *Welsh Rugby Captains* (Gomer, 2010).

—, *St. Helen's Stories* (Gomer, 2007).

Billot, John, *History of Welsh International Rugby* (Roman Way, 1999).

Cole, Rob and Stuart Farmer, *Wales Rugby Miscellany* (Vision Sports, 2008).

Davies, Gareth and Terry Goodwin, *Standing Off,* (Queen Anne, 1986).

Davies, D.E., *Cardiff R.F.C 1876–1975* (Cardiff Athletic Club, 1975).

Davies, Gerald, *An Autobiography* (Allen and Unwin, 1979).

Davies, Jonathan with Peter Corrigan *An Autobiography* (Stanley Paul, 1989).

Davis, Jack, *One Hundred Years of Newport Rugby Club* (Starling, 1974).

Edwards, Gareth, *100 Great Rugby Players* (Macmillan, 1987).

—, *The Autobiography* (Headline, 2000).

Edwards, Gareth and Peter Bills, *Tackling Rugby: The Changing World of Professional Rugby* (Headline, 2002).

Evans, Alan and Duncan Gardiner, *Cardiff R.F.C 1940–2000* (Stroud Tempus, 2000).

Evans, Alan, *Taming the Toursits* (Vertical Edition, 2003).

—, *The Dragons Who Roared* (Daffodil, 2006).

Evans, Howard, *Welsh International Matches, 1881–2011* (Y Lolfa, 2011).

Evans, Ieuan with Peter Jackson, *Bread of Heaven* (Mainstream, 1995).

Farmer, David, *The All Whites:the Life and Times of Swansea RFC* (DFPS, 1995).

Gate, Robert, *Gone North*, Vols 1 and 2 (Gate, 1986, 1988).

Jackson, Peter, *Lions of Wales: A Celebration of Welsh Rugby Legends* (Mainstream, 1998).

James, Royston, *Can Llwyddiant* (Christopher Davies, 1981).

Jenkins, John, *CARWYN Un o 'fois y pentre'* (Gomer, 1983).

Jenkins, Neil with Paul Rees, *Life at Number 10* (Mainstream, 1998).

Jenkins, Pierce and Auty, *Who's Who of Welsh International Rugby* (Bridge, 1991).

John, Barry and Paul Abbandonato, *The King* (Mainstream, 1981).

John, Barry and Clem Thomas, *Rugby Wales '87* (Christopher Davies, 1986).

Jones, Robert, *Raising the Dragon* (Virgin, 2001).

Keating, Frank, *The Great Number Tens* (Partridge, 1983).

Lawrie, W.A.D., *Bridgend R.F.C. – The First 100 Years* (Bridgend R.F.C, 1979).

Lewis, Steve, *The Priceless Gift: 125 Years of Welsh Rugby Captains* (Mainstream, 2006).

—, *Newport RFC 1874–1950* (Tempus, 1999).

—, *Newport RFC 1950–2000* (Orbiting, 2000).

Morgan, Cliff, *The Autobiography – Beyond the Fields of Play* (Hodder and Stoughton, 1996).

Morris, Graham, *Salford City Reds* (Vertical Editions, 2002).

Parry-Jones, David, *Taff's Acre* (Collins, 1984).

—, *Out of the Ruck* (Pelham, 1986).

—, *The Rugby Clubs of Wales* (Hutchison, 1989).

—, *The Gwilliam Seasons* (Seren, 2003).

—, *The Dawes Decades* (Seren, 2005).

Price, Mike, *Neath RFC 1945–1996* (The History Press, 2004).

Reason, John, *Victorious Lions* (Rugby Books, 1971).

—, *The Unbeaten Lions* (Rugby Books, 1974).

—, *Lions Down Under* (Rugby Books, 1977).

—, *Backs to the Wall* (Rugby Books, 1980).

Reason, John and Carwyn James, *The World of Rugby: A History of RU Football* (BBC, 1979).

Richards, Alun, *A Touch of Glory* (Michael Joseph, 1980).

Richards, Huw, *Dragons and All Blacks* (Mainstream, 2004).

—, *A Game for Hooligans* (Mainstream, 2007).

Richards, Huw, Peter Stead and Gareth Williams (eds), *Heart and Soul* (University of Wales Press, 1998).

—, *More Heart and Soul* (University of Wales Press, 1999).

Ring, Mark with Delme Parfitt, *Ringmaster* (Mainstream, 2006).

Roderick, Alan, *Newport Rugby Greats* (Handpost, 1995).

Rowlands, Clive and David Farmer (eds), *Giants of Post-War Welsh Rugby* (Malcolm Press, 1990).

Rowlands, Clive and John Evans, *Clive* (Gomer, 2000).

Smith, David B. and Gareth W. Williams, *Fields of Praise* (University of Wales Press, 1981).

Thomas, Clem and Geoffrey Nicholson, *The Crowning Years* (Collins, 1980).

Thomas, J.B.G., *The Lions on Trek* (Stanley Paul, 1956).

—, *Great Contemporary Players* (Stanley Paul, 1963).

—, *The Men in Scarlet* (Pelham, 1972).

—, *The Illustrated History of Welsh Rugby* (Pelham, 1980).

—, *Rugger in the Blood: Fifty Years of Rugby Memoirs* (Pelham, 1985).

Thomas, Wayne, *A Century of Welsh Rugby Players 1880–1980* (Ansells, 1980).

Watkins, David with Brian Dobbs, *The David Watkins Story* (Pelham, 1971).

Westcott, Gordon, *A Century on the Rugby Beat* (South Wales Police R.F.C., 1992).

Williams, Bleddyn, *Rugger My Life* (Stanley Paul, 1956).

Williams, Gareth, *The First Fifteen* (Parthian, 2011).

Williams, J.P.R., *J.P.R: The Autobiography* (Collins, 1979).

Windsor, Bobby and Peter Jackson, *The Iron Duke* (Mainstream, 2010).

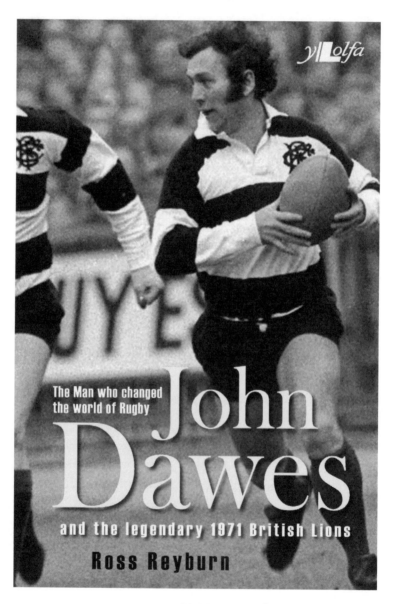

The Man who changed
the world of Rugby

John
Dawes

and the legendary 1971 British Lions

Ross Reyburn

£9.95

STEVE LEWIS

All Black
and
Amber

1963 and a Game of Rugby

When Newport
beat New Zealand

y Lolfa

£9.95

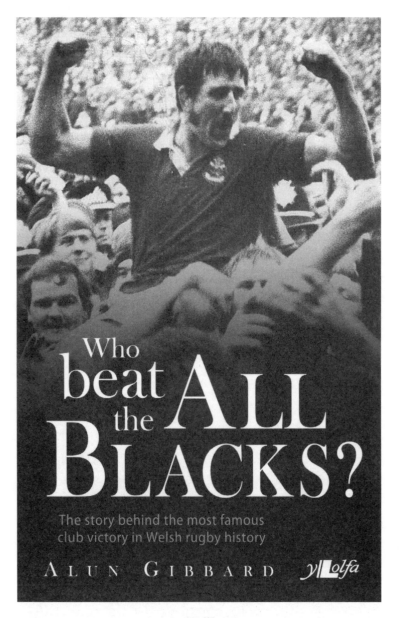

Who
beat ALL
the
BLACKS?

The story behind the most famous
club victory in Welsh rugby history

ALUN GIBBARD

y Lolfa

£9.95

LYNN DAVIES

hard men
of WELSH
RUGBY

y Lolfa

£7.95